ANXIOUS TO AWESOME

A PRACTICAL GUIDE
FOR THE WHOLE FAMILY

Mira Binzen, C-IAYT

Global Family Press

PO Box 424

Ames, IA 50010

Ordering Information:

Quantity sales. Special discounts are available on quantity purchases by corporations, associations, and others. For details, contact the "Special Sales Department" at the address above.

Anxious to Awesome; Mira Binzen. —1st ed.

ISBN 979-8-9854019-0-5

Anxiety is the number one mental health challenge in the world today – for both kids and adults. When it seems like life stirs up anxious feelings at nearly every turn, it may feel like a distant dream to feel awesome or even at ease. This practical guidebook is for families who want to feel less anxious and more awesome without a huge investment of time or money.

Table of Contents

Welcome

Hello and welcome. I am so glad you're here. Everyone deserves to feel vibrant, connected and at ease. That's what awesome means to me. What I'm going to share with you in this book can help you feel awesome too. I want to make it simple for you and easy to do. I'm the tour guide on your journey from anxious to awesome.

One of the most awesome experiences of my life was learning to ride a bike. I'll never forget it! My older sister, Stephanie, and I were on the sidewalk across the street from our house. I had one of those banana-seat bikes with streamers at the ends of the handlebars. It was an orange bike and the seat was covered with big bright flowers. I steadied myself on the seat with my sister firmly hanging on to the rounded bar at the back. I pushed my foot against one pedal. Then, I put my other foot on the other pedal and started to move. I was wobbly at first, but she was there to support me. My sister, who's always been at my side, ran alongside as I road down the whole block. My hair and the streamers were flying back in the wind. Such freedom! Such joy!

I pushed the pedals in reverse to stop the bike at the end of the block and put my foot down on the hot summer sidewalk. I turned around and was surprised to see my sister wasn't there! She stopped running several houses back when she saw I was steady on my own. I couldn't believe I had done it all by myself. I thought my sister was still holding on.

My mind allowed me to stay balanced on my bike! I was thrilled. Thank you, Stephanie.

To this day, riding a bike is one of my favorite things to do. I love the freedom. I love to feel the change in air temperature as I ride under a canopy of trees. I love to weave around rocks and cracks in the sidewalks and I love to lean into turns. I love getting where I'm going under my own power.

This is what I want to teach you – how to get where you want to go under your own power. I'm going to teach you to be the captain of your ship. I'll be at your side until you get underway on your own sails. You may not believe you can, but you're more capable than you know. Just like me on that first solo bike ride.

I was an anxious kid. Sometimes I'm still an anxious adult. But I've got tools and a lifestyle that help me handle it with grace. And now you will too.

I've been interested in the mind since I was in 9th grade. The first time I learned about psychology in school something in me lit up. It was exciting and seemed familiar. I dove in. I was lucky enough to have a great library at the end of my block where I could find so many interesting books about it. Let's hear it for awesome library systems! I learned that people thousands of years ago were very interested in the mind as well. They mapped out the processes in the mind and created a system for developing a healthy mind. What I learned made so much sense and gave me a deep feeling of recognition. It's been my life's passion ever since.

Since high school, I've worked with children with disabilities, trauma and mental health concerns like anxiety. As an adult, I worked as a Yoga therapist at Minneapolis Children's Integrative Medicine clinic. There, I helped children just like you manage anxious feelings that came with their medical challenges or an upcoming big surgery. If you've ever had to go to the hospital, you know how stressful it can be. I also helped families who were spending long days in the hospital with their ill children. I shared with them the same tools I'm going to share with you.

It's easy to understand and simple to use.

For more than 12 years, I've been teaching a series of classes I named "Anxious to Awesome™". I'm delighted to share what I've learned with you in this book. It's a practical guidebook for families. I've written it so more people can use and benefit from these tools that make a big difference in how you feel each day. It's easy to understand and simple to use.

What is Anxiety?

First of all, as a person with anxious feelings, you're not alone. Look around you anytime, anywhere. Up to half the people you see have anxious feelings on a regular basis. We all do sometimes. Then, there are all the folks at home you can't see because they feel too anxious to go out. Anxiety is the number one mental health challenge in the world today.

Anxiety is your body's intelligence hitting the alarm to keep you safe. Sometimes, it pulls the fire alarm when there is no fire. Or, the alarm gets stuck in the "ON" position. Anxiety is both a psychological (mind) and a physiological (body) state. Your mind worries and your tummy is upset. Anxiety can come from inside or outside, or both. There are many kinds of anxiety.

- Panic is when feelings of fright strike suddenly. You may or may not be in a frightening situation when this happens.
- Post-traumatic stress (PTSD) may develop following a distressing event or series of events. The scary situation has passed but the scary feelings are still there.
- Some people have an intense fear of something specific. This is called a phobia. Fear of heights and snakes are common phobias.

- Social anxiety involves overwhelming worry about everyday social situations, like going to school or a concert or participating in afterschool activities.
- Obsessive and compulsive behavior (OCD) happens when a ritual or routine must be performed, many times, to feel safe and to keep something bad from happening.
- Generalized anxiety means that whether you are in a stressful situation or not, you still feel anxious.

These all have the same effect on the body and mind. Long-term exposure to stressful situations and/or chronic stress can disrupt nearly every system in the body.

There are many signs that you may be dealing with stress and anxiety. Different people experience different emotional, physical, mental and behavioral symptoms. Do any of these seem familiar?

You feel:

- Like hiding in your room and avoiding people/situations
- Overwhelmed and out of control
- Easily agitated, frustrated, and moody
- Negative about yourself/depressed/lonely
- Frequently worried
- Hopeless about the future

You have:

- Frequent headaches and/or stomachaches
- Low energy
- Sweaty palms
- Grinding teeth
- Restless sleep/can't sleep

- Racing thoughts
- Difficulty focusing
- Changes in your appetite – overeating or not eating
- Nervous habits such as nail biting, hair twirling, fidgeting or pacing

When I experience anxiety, it feels to me like someone has hijacked my brain. This character called "anxiety" has snuck up from behind and is holding me hostage. It's a weird feeling because it's often not directly related to something that's happening in that moment. What does it feel like to you? Make some notes in a journal. I'll tell you about keeping a captain's log later in this chapter.

The definition of, and ways to address anxiety keeps changing. But you will always be you, and you can practice being the best version of you every day. You can start anytime and go anywhere you like.

What is Awesome?

Your life is a journey. On this journey you'll have many experiences. When going on an adventure, it's fun to think about what it's like when you get to your destination. We're going on an adventure from anxious to awesome, so let's begin with the end in mind. What is awesome?

Awesome is a big word. Awesome is something that takes your breath away. It's astounding and astonishing, stunning and amazing. And isn't that exactly what life is?

- A rollercoaster ride
- Hitting the ball outta the park
- Helping a friend in need
- A perfect launch with your model rocket
- Getting to the next level of your game

- Locking in that last piece of a puzzle
- Seeing your new baby brother smile
- Biting into a perfectly ripe peach, or your grandma's perfect peach pie

The stressors and pressures of day-to-day life can rob us of these awesome moments. Once you learn that you've got your hand on the controls, you'll have everyday awesome. You'll be the captain of your ship and not the passenger.

And even the moments that are not so awesome like:

- Falling and skinning your knee – in front of your friends
- Doing not-so-great on a test
- Listening to your parents fight
- Feeling overwhelmed by a new situation

You'll be able to be with these moments and still be okay. Life is a river, it's always flowing, always changing. Sometimes the river is calm and wide. Other times, it's a turbulent jumble of chaotic energy. In this book, my friend, you are learning to navigate the big waters of life with skill, grace and ease.

To me, feeling awesome has a lot to do with being the captain of my own ship. That means I can make empowered choices. I am in control. I set the sails.

- I feel confident in the ship's mechanics (my body)
- I know how to set the sails (breathe well)
- I am a good navigator (strong mind)
- I know about the wildlife in the sea and the stars in the sky (nature)
- I also have a great crew onboard (people)

What does awesome feel like to you? It's okay if you don't know yet. This can take some time. Daydream, talk with friends and family, keep a journal. Have fun with the activities and tools in this guidebook as you discover your own awesome.

How to go from Anxious to Awesome

There are two main ways you can feel less anxious and more awesome. One is to have more awareness. Awareness means paying attention. It's like a flashlight you shine on something to see it better. It's one of those cool flashlights that you can twist in for sharp focus or twist out for a big floodlight effect. The more you pay attention, the more awesome you'll feel. It doesn't mean perfect. It means a clearer picture and a bigger view. So when you do feel anxious, you can be more understanding and loving to yourself. You can be with anxious feelings, as they are. You may also choose to nudge yourself toward feeling a tiny bit better. Awareness also leads to empowered choices.

Awareness also leads to empowered choices.

The second way to feel less anxious and more awesome is connection. That means you feel good when you feel part of it all. At the root of feeling unwell – in the body or the mind – is a sense of being alone or apart. The tools in this guidebook are tools to help you reconnect with your body, breath, mind, nature and people.

The books I was checking out from the library on the science of mind were about awareness and connection. It's like cleaning the windshield on the car you're driving for a better view. And, having your hands on the steering wheel while understanding all the dials on the dashboard. Okay, when you're a driver, there will be a screen instead of dials and you may not even need to keep your hands on the wheel! But you get what I'm saying, right?

Since ancient times, people have wondered about and wanted what was best in life. A word I like to use for this is "thrive". It means to be your best and feel your best. Traditional cultures all had a way of being well that was deeply connected to nature. People spent most of the time outside in nature and used plants for medicine as well as food. There was also an element of mindfulness or awareness in this ancient wisdom. Paying attention was a matter of survival.

Humans evolved and gained super-cool technology like computers and space travel. Yet, we have to be careful that this outer technology doesn't erode or hide our inner technology of self-awareness, self-regulation and self-mastery. Self-awareness is understanding what's going on inside you – your body and your mind. Self-regulation is putting on the captain's hat. You stand on the captain's deck and steer the ship to stay on course, or to get back on course. You understand the controls and know how to operate them. Self-mastery is when you've been the captain of your own ship for a while. You know how to sail through a storm. And you also know where the best beaches are.

How to Use This Guidebook

You are holding in your hands a guidebook to awesome. In this guide, I'll be sharing tools and activities that you get to choose from and use how you like. As a family, you can help each other remember the tools and use them when you're feeling anxious or lost on this amazing journey called "life".

The tools in this guidebook can help you with any type of anxiety. You may take this book to your favorite corner to read and do the activities by yourself, like I did when I was a kid. Or, your parent or a favorite grown-up can read it to you. Along with this book, you may need professional support from a doctor or therapist. It's a team effort. You'll learn how to take care of yourself and have others who can help take care of you too.

> I'll include some notes to grown-ups too. In a gray box like this. You may want to read through the book and filter out the parts you think will be most appealing and helpful for your child. Read those sections to your child and do the activities together. I bet you'll also appreciate using some of these tools for yourself.

There are five areas we will focus on. Areas to be more aware and connected.

- Body
- Breath
- Mind
- Nature
- People

Moving your body with awareness, shaping your breath, tending to your mind, engaging with nature and with others will help you feel better. Sometimes a little bit and often a lot. There is a chapter for each area. You can think of each of these chapters like a menu. Pick the tools in the chapters that look good to you. If you try something and it helps you feel less anxious, there's no need to keep trying other tools unless you want to. Different tools work differently for each person. Pick one tool from each chapter – body, breath, mind, nature and people – to play with each day. When you're feeling anxious, you may need to try several tools in a row to find relief. You'll find what works for you.

You may be a person who loves variety and novelty. You want to try all the things! Go ahead. Or, you may like things to be familiar and routine. You'll discover three to five tools you can visit over and over again like old friends. I'll help you make a plan in Chapter 7 on Practice.

The last chapter of this book, Everyday Awesome, ties it all together. This becomes a way of being. Just like you have your own unique wardrobe, you'll have your own unique tools and routines for feeling awesome.

These tools are based on an ancient science of the mind and a deep understanding of nature – your own nature and the natural world around you.

This is a discovery process. You can discover the precious gem of the real you that may be hidden behind an anxious mind or a too frenetic life. There's nothing you need to add or go find or "fix". It's already within you. You'll get spy glasses, a compass, maps, special tools, secret keys, flashlights and a life jacket…so to speak.

The last thing you want to hear when you're feeling anxious is that you should "get over it". Or that "it's all in your head" or, anything that can help you is "easy". Anxiety is a complex condition.

Having said that, you may find many of the tools in this book are enjoyable. You may find you can do them in a few minutes. And, you might start feeling better right away. You may also find that over time, you are learning a new way of being with yourself and the world. You may find yourself feeling a little more awesome.

"Except when you *don't*", as Dr. Seuss says in the book, *Oh, The Places You'll Go.*

"Because, sometimes, you won't.

I'm sorry to say so

but, sadly, it's true

that Bang-ups

and Hang-ups

can happen to you."

When Bang-ups happen, you'll feel more like the pilot than the passenger. You'll pull yourself out of that tailspin and right the plane…or know when it's time to hit the eject button and parachute outta there. You'll discover your own personal power and a sense of freedom that's always inside you.

Captain's Log

You're on an adventure. It may be helpful to chart your course, to keep track of where you've been and where you're going. And, to capture insights and "ahas" along the way. Make your own journal. It can be as simple as a few blank pieces of paper and your favorite box of colored pencils or a spiral notebook from the dollar store. Get something fancier if you like. Decorate it, name it, keep it safe. Or just use the captain's log pages in this book.

Keep a written journal or daily drawings to help you get to know your mind and your habits. Write down feelings and even make them characters in a story to help you step back and be the observer. Mr. Moody or Anxious Annie can become a character in your life rather than an overwhelming mental state. This ability is a powerful life skill that helps you be aware of difficult feelings without being consumed by them.

Online Resources

Bring this guidebook to life with additional resources you will find online. Wherever you see "online resources" you can go to: www.anxioustoawesome.com/familyresources. You'll find video and audio of some of the tools, along with colorful pictures of nature art and friends along the way. It's here where you can also connect with me and share some notes or pictures from your journey. I'd love to hear from you!

Let's Get Science-y!

We're going to get a bit science-y too. It's a mash up of the old and the new. The ancient masters of the science of the mind knew this stuff. They experimented on themselves. Through the power of attention and insight, they developed many of the tools in this book. It's like a 2,000-year-old case study. Now, neuroscientists can measure the brain and the movement of the mind like never before. Cutting-edge imaging techniques are proving in a lab what people have been teaching for thousands of years.

When I was young, I had vivid dreams. Each one was like an epic movie. Over the years, I would try to share my dreams with my mom or a friend. I got frustrated standing in the kitchen in my pink fuzzy slippers on a Saturday morning trying to describe the feeling, the colors, the scene to my mom – all of it. I decided I needed to invent a dream screen to solve my frustration. This would be a device that you could hook your brain up to so you could project your dream onto a screen for others to see. I was pretty excited about this idea. But when I discovered how many years of science I would need to study to be able to invent this, I realized this was not the route for me. I was more interested in working directly with people. I got to volunteer at a school for children with disabilities and continued to learn about the mind and human behavior.

The science in this book is intentionally simplified, so someone like me – with not too much training in science and a lot of interest in people – can understand. You'll also learn more about what's happening when anxious feelings hijack your brain and what you can do to get your brain back on track.

We're trying to understand something very complex, that's not easily measured. You can put your brain on a scale and weigh it. It's about three pounds. But trying to measure what it does, well, that's like trying to colonize Mars. Scientists are busy attempting to do both!

You can understand the basic mechanics of your brain and learn simple tools to impact it. You are the pilot. You truly are in control. The science-y sections are a way to learn the instrumentation of your vessel.

> *The science-y sections are a way to learn the*
> *instrumentation of your vessel.*

Some of you are jumping up and down right now. "Yay, science!" Others may have just thumped the palm of your hand to your forehead. "Oh no, not more science." Maybe science is a hard subject for you in school or you don't have a natural buzz in your body around the subject of science. That's cool. You are welcome to dive in as deep as you like. You can just dip your toe in the water and read little bits of Let's Get Science-y! Then jump right into the stories and tools in the chapters. Come back later and read a bit more when you feel like it. The tools themselves will help you better understand and experience the awesomely cool science of YOU.

Those of you still jumping up and down? You'll devour all the sections and be hungry for more. Go ahead and do more research. Neuroscience is an exciting new field. You could be the one to make a new discovery about how the brain works.

You'll know we're done being Science-y! when you see this symbol.

Friends Along the Way

You'll meet several kids in this book who have taken the journey from anxious to awesome. Names and identifying details of some of these kids have been changed. Their stories will be in italics. You'll learn what these kids have done, and you can do the same things too. I hope you can relate to their stories and that they inspire you on your journey. Like Hannah.

I hope you can relate to their stories and that they inspire you on your journey.

~ /~ ~

Hannah's anxiety started in 7ᵗʰ grade. All her classes had changed. She used to have several friends. And now, there wasn't anyone she knew in her classes. Lunch was the worst. She had a fear of being judged. Her grades plummeted. To make things worse, a boy in her class made up a story about her that wasn't true. The other kids teased her relentlessly about this lie. Going to school each day became a major source of stress.

Hannah says, "That year was kinda rough. It was definitely odd. It was really, really difficult for me. It was like having to make friends again. I didn't really know how to do it. It was very anxiety inducing to lose all my friends and then have to make new friends."

In the 8th grade, she was diagnosed with a brain tumor. At the time, the treatment needed or the outcome wasn't known. "Honestly, that was a weird one" she shared. "That was absolutely terrifying for me. As a kid with anxiety to actually have a brain tumor in my head, aack! Where do I even go from there! For a solid couple of months, I thought I was dying. The MRIs were something I had to breathe through and center myself." Fortunately, she had been practicing tools you'll learn in this book so this was easier to do during this stressful time.

~ ~ ~

Riley was nine years old when she first took the series of classes called, Anxious to Awesome™. Like Hannah, school was a major source of stress for her. She did well with her schoolwork but struggled with the other kids in her class. When she felt anxious, some kids would tease her about it, making it worse.

She learned the same tools you'll learn in this book. She started feeling better. At the end of one class, after being guided to relax, everyone got to share how they were feeling. When it was her turn, she pushed her glasses back up the bridge of her nose and said, "I don't know if this is even possible! I feel energized AND relaxed."

It is possible and this is my wish for you. These tools of connection and awareness can help you feel a focused calm, an energized stability, just like Riley.

~ ~ ~

Can you relate to either of these stories? What's your story? Write it down. How are you feeling right now? What's causing your anxious feelings? It could be something happening in your life. It could also be a general feeling that you can't pinpoint. This is your baseline, your starting point. Write the date down too. You can come back later and see how far you've come.

The easy-to-use tools in this guidebook can help you feel better in all areas of your life. It's not a prescription, a treatment or a cure. It's a lifestyle of being in tune with and connected to all of life around you on a day-to-day basis.

Captain's Log

Chapter 1 – Stress or Rest

"Almost everything will work again if you unplug it for a few minutes...Including you."

~ Anne Lamott

I like to think of stress, anxiety and panic on a scale – like a Laugh-O-Meter, only not so funny. It's different for everyone. What is stressful for you, may not be for another. Something that provokes anxiety in someone else may be no big deal to you. Anxious feelings often aren't related to a specific situation. It can be a function of how your brain works. At the end of this chapter, I'll show you how to make your own Stress-O-Meter so you can rate how you are feeling. This can help you take action.

Nervous System

Your nervous system is the main communication system in your body. Within it is the autonomic nervous system (ANS). It works "autonomously", which means you never have to think about it. It runs millions of processes in your body like:

- Digest food
- Maintain body temperature
- Manage immunity
- Regulate heart rate and blood pressure
- All while building and repairing cells

There are two sides to your ANS. One side, the sympathetic side, helps you be energized, focused and alert. It helps you pay attention in school and jump out of the road to avoid an oncoming car. It prepares you to run across the soccer field and score a goal. It's like a movie director calling "action!" The sympathetic nervous system is meant to address a specific situation for a short time.

When this system is engaged, the body releases adrenaline and other hormones that trigger a whole set of responses. This prepares the body for the emergency or activity at hand. Heart rate and blood pressure increase. Muscles tighten. (Are your muscles tight right now?) Pupils dilate and the senses become sharper – so you can take the action needed to survive or to make that goal. You become stronger, faster and more focused.

The other side of the ANS is the parasympathetic nervous system. This system helps your body return to balance after an alarming or exciting situation. I remember this one by thinking "parachute". Ahhh, time to relax. This is when the director calls "cut!" In this mode the body focuses on resting, rebuilding, repairing and digesting. None of this can happen when you're stressed out.

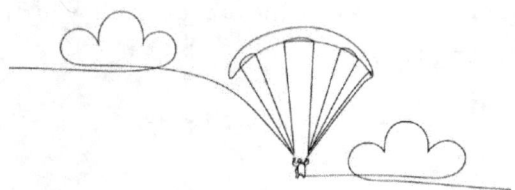

Once the emergency has passed or you've won the soccer game and are getting ready for bed, the body is meant to return to this "rest and digest" mode. This system is engaged when the outside environment is perceived as calm. It slows the heartbeat and stimulates digestion so the body can get back to routine tasks.

It's one or the other. This is the wisdom of your body. Your body doesn't waste energy having all the functions going at once. It shifts in response to current needs. Like the lights in your house. You turn the lights on where you need them, not throughout the whole house. Your brain and body are energy efficient.

Stress side = action, alarm, safety

Rest side = rest, digest, build and repair

Unfortunately, low-grade stress seems to pervade our lives. All the lights in the house get left on. You may never fully drop into this essential rest and digest response. The flood of hormones so essential to your survival in acutely stressful situations becomes toxic to your system when it's chronic. These powerful hormones and the stress response they trigger can cause significant damage to physical and mental health.

Stress can get in the way of learning and memory. Studies have shown that the chemicals released in the body during times of stress alter the hippocampus, the area of the brain responsible for memory and learning. Long-term stress can even rewire the brain, leaving you more vulnerable to anxiety and depression.

~ ~ ~

Hanna struggled with depression as well as anxiety and her grades started to suffer. She recalled a specific example of this. "The first time I got a C on a math test, I lost it." She said, "I was freaking out. I had to go into the bathroom because I started having a panic attack."

~ ~ ~

If you don't learn to manage anxious feelings when young, you may be more susceptible to harmful stress throughout your life. Do you know people who seem unable to cope with everyday challenges or who have a hard time adapting to new situations? It is likely their stress-hardiness has been eroded over time by constant bombardment of stress hormones in their system.

It is not possible, or even recommended, to completely eliminate stress. A certain amount of stress is okay – it's actually helpful. Better focus, strength, stamina and being more alert are exactly what you need sometimes. Like when taking a test or scoring a goal on the soccer field.

When you feel chronic stress or anxiety it means that instead of switching back and forth as needed, the alarm mode got stuck in the "ON" position. But guess what? You can partner with the wisdom of your body to help shift from stress mode to rest mode. That's what this book is all about. Simple tools you can use on your own to shift out of stress and into rest.

True story. I spin fire. I've been on stage with a live band in front of thousands of people. One time, I was on stage for about five minutes. Big crowd cheering, colored lights flashing and fire flying past my head. Everyone was having so much fun, but my brain was interpreting all this as a big emergency. My nervous system was in alarm mode! When I left the stage, I had to walk around and breathe deeply for more than an hour to burn off all the adrenaline that built up. I didn't use it for an emergency so those chemicals built up in my body stayed there. They caused a stomachache, racing heart and a nervous, fidgeting feeling. This same chemical process happens when you spend days worrying about a test, your family's health or the state of the world.

At the beginning of this chapter, I mentioned that you can think of stress, anxiety and panic on a scale – like a Laugh-O-Meter, only not so funny. The first step in taking action to feel better is to know how you feel in the first place. You can rate your anxious feelings on the Stress-O-Meter. Remember, it's different for everyone.

When anxiety hits, it can feel like it's always a ten on a scale of one-to-ten. With this meter, you'll better understand how you are feeling inside and that there can be a range. There are degrees of anxious feelings. It may be a ten in intensity, or it may be a six, or a three. You'll learn to recognize your anxious feelings when they are less than a ten on the meter and it will be easier to do something about it.

Share your current rating on your Stress-O-Meter with a caring adult. It can help them help you. Or, make some notes in your captain's log.

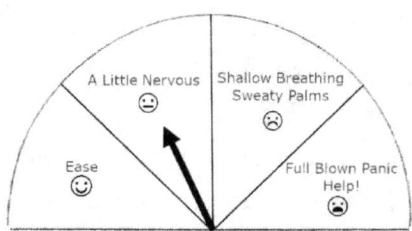

Make Your Own Stress-O-Meter

Supplies: Piece of paper, markers, split pin and a plate

Trace a half circle on the paper, using a plate as your guide. Draw a line straight down the middle. Then draw two more lines to split these halves in half, one on each side of the middle line. Color each section. Green = ease. Yellow = a little nervous. Orange = shallow breathing, sweaty palms. Red = full blown anxiety. Please help! You can choose the words and colors you use for your meter. Cut out an arrow shape and attach it to the base of your meter with a stick pin. Move the arrow to the section that best describes your current level of anxious feelings.

Try some tools in this book and check the meter again and see if it goes down. Always please seek help when you need it, especially when you find yourself rating your anxious feelings on the high end of the Stress-O-Meter.

Okay, captain-in-training! You're starting to collect and learn how to use tools to chart your course from anxious to awesome. In each of the next chapters, we'll focus on an area to be connected and aware. Next up, Body.

Captain's Log

Chapter 2 – Body

"An anxious mind cannot exist in a relaxed body."

~ Dr. Edmund Jacobson

When was the last time you thought about your body? I mean, reaalllly thought about it? It's astonishing. There are trillions of processes going on in your body right now. You don't even have to think about it. It just happens. The human body is miraculous. It knows what to do all on its own. There is an intelligence that keeps things humming along. All the actions in your body have the single purpose of keeping you alive and well. This is called homeostasis. That's a fancy word for "balance". Your body will work very hard to come back into balance every time.

Everything you do, eat and think either helps your body be in balance or gets in the way of it being in balance. The tools in this chapter promote balance (homeostasis). There are many simple things you can do every day to help your body be well. Living in a balanced body is awesome!

There are many simple things you can do every day to help your body be well.

Movement also helps reduce anxiety. Physical tension in the body is a common symptom of anxiety. Releasing tension can release anxiety. Physical activity can counteract the effects of stress.

Let's Get Science-y!

This book focuses on the science of your brain and nervous system. Did you know you have a brain in your belly? It's called the enteric nervous system. Sometimes it's called your second brain or "gut brain". Your gut brain has more neurons (nerve cells) than your spine! Scientists didn't pay much attention to it at first. But now, it seems that serotonin, a feel-good chemical that plays a big role in good moods, is produced in the enteric nervous system. More than 90% of serotonin is manufactured here. Butterflies in your tummy? That's your enteric nervous system.

Doctors used to think that anxious feelings can cause an upset stomach. Now, researchers think it may be the other way around. An imbalance in this gut brain could be causing anxious feelings in the mind. Some researchers think one cause of anxiety may be lower levels of serotonin. For this reason, it's important to have good gut health. The activities in this chapter can help keep this area healthy, especially Easy Twist. In the next chapter, you'll learn about breathing in a way that can also help. You are meant to be well. You are meant to live in a relaxed and comfortable body.

You are meant to be well. You are meant to live in a relaxed and comfortable body.

These are my favorite ways to take care of my body. Try them and find your own favorites. Pick one or two to start. Come back later for more. In the chapter on Practice, we'll weave together different tools so you can see how it all works in your day.

Pay attention to how you feel before you try these tools. And then notice how you feel after. These are things you can do every day, when you're feeling anxious or, better yet, before you feel anxious. Keep some notes in your captain's log.

Your body is a kaleidoscope of information. This information comes in the form of "sensation". You feel a rumbling in your belly when you are hungry. You may feel like there's a ball of lead in it when you fail a test. That zingy excited feeling that starts in your belly and rushes up through your body? That's excitement…or fear…or something else. Everyone has their own feelings. Yours may be different from mine, but we all have them.

One day I was sitting in my Special Place. (I'll tell you more about this in the chapter on Practice). The thought came to me, "I'm happy." Then I wondered, "How do I know I'm happy?" I checked the sensations in my body to find out what happy feels like. The words that popped up were "buoyant, calm". My body felt quiet and steady. It also felt like a ginormous colorful hot air balloon ready to take off with all the people I love on board.

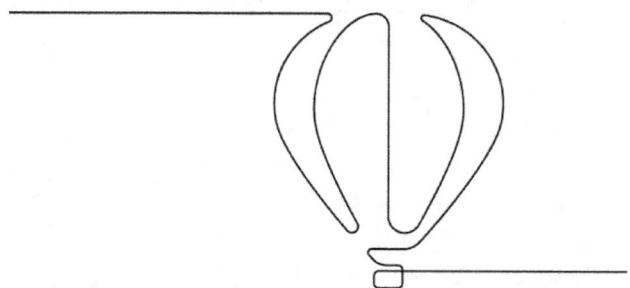

Name It!

"Name It!" is a fun activity the whole family can play. Help each other learn to be more familiar with these messages, or "sensations" from your body. The reason you want to get to know these messages is because they guide you. Your body gives you signals. Learning your body signals can give you a big head start in managing anxious feelings. It's like getting a tip something is about to happen before it happens. You become the meteorologist of yourself. You learn to detect a storm coming from off in the distance and can plan for it.

Learning your body signals can give you a big head start in managing anxious feelings.

Next time someone says, "I feel (tired, hungry, excited, mad, bored)." Ask them where they feel it in their body. What is the sensation they are aware of that makes them say how they are feeling? Where is this feeling born in the body?

The truth is, at first, this can be super annoying. Because often you don't know. But, if your family has agreed to do this in the spirit of feeling more awesome, then you are ready for the question. At first, you'll say something like, "Huh, I don't know." But when you are patient and pay attention, you'll start to notice different feelings in your body that relate to states in your mind. This is one way you can manage your anxious feelings.

It's like walking into a darkened room. At first, you can't see anything. As you spend more time in the room and your eyes adjust, you start to make out some shapes. Then after some time, you can see even more.

If you have chronic pain, a medical condition or a physical disability, you may think about your body all the time. It may be a part of why you have anxious feelings. Your body may communicate with you more, or differently, or in some areas, not at all.

I've been teaching families about how to live well in their body for many years. Someone who taught me a lot about this is Matthew Sanford. He has been paralyzed since he was 13 years old. He now teaches body awareness to people with physical disabilities. He teaches them to listen very carefully to their body. There's an energy – a hum or a buzz – that you can tune into even when the signal lines are down, as is the case with paralysis.

Matthew told me once that, in some ways, it's harder for me to learn about body awareness than him because I have an "easy" body. He *needs* to pay closer attention to do physical things like morning stretches so it makes him more aware. You have an opportunity to befriend your body, however it is. A feeling of wellbeing can be experienced by anyone in any body.

To "Name It!", it can be helpful to start with a menu of sensations you can say "yes" or "no" to. Here are some examples:

soft   sinking   hot   loose   thick
slippery dull   hard   rough   puffy
tingly quiet cold tight   heavy
spinny   light   sharp   fluffy   dry
zingy   fast comfortable   floating
spacious   comfortable   itchy

Another common response to this question of "Where do you feel an emotion or experience in your body?" is "Everywhere!"

~ ~ ~

That's what seven-year-old Jackson said. His brother had just pushed him down as they walked into their after-school program causing his new Pokémon backpack to twist off his back and fall to the floor. The tension had been building up for a while before they came in. His brother teased him for spilling milk at breakfast and he tripped him on the way to the bus. If you have a brother or sister, you can probably relate.

He was angry and said so. He was learning these same tools you are in this book. He had some practice exploring the kaleidoscope of information in his body and knew the "Name It!" game.

Me: Hey, Jackson! What's up?

Jackson: I'm angry!!

Me: Where do you feel that in your body?

Jackson: Everywhere!!!

Anger is a big, strong emotion. It can feel like it's taking over the whole body. I gave him some options, like a menu, to pinpoint the sensations a bit.

34

Me: Do you feel it in your big toe? Do you feel it at the tip of your nose?

Jackson: No and no.

Me: Do you feel it in your belly?

Jackson: Yes!

Then, he could describe it.

Me: Tell me more.

Jackson: It's hot, heavy, moving fast.

Locating and describing the sensation was enough to help him feel less angry. Instead of the anger driving him, "Name It!" put him back in the driver's seat.

~ ~ ~

This practice is like learning a new language. It can take some time, but the more you do it, the more fluently you and your body can talk. This is called *body awareness*. You are aware of your body inside and out. You are "embodied". That means you are living in your body, and you can feel it.

It's common in this high-tech, outward-focused world to not pay much attention to the body. We live in our heads. When you do pay attention to your body, you will learn a lot. It may enhance your experience of being human, in a big way. In other words, being you feels awesome.

Now, this is the important part. Being more aware of your body can help you feel less anxious. Total body awareness and anxiety are not compatible. Learning to pay attention to sensations in your body is a powerful tool for feeling less anxious. It also helps you notice anxious feelings sooner, so you can choose a tool in this book and shift out of it before it takes over. Every day, and even every hour, do something to help you feel and know and live in your body.

Every day, and even every hour, do something to help you feel and know and live in your body.

Your body is always talking to you. You can stop and listen any time. Sometimes the message is loud enough that you stop and take notice. Other times, you may just want to check in. "Hey, body", you can say, "What's up"? The body is like a gorgeous palace. You can go room by room to see the luxurious furnishings, beautiful art and nice porcelain vases. Explore your palace. You may find something. Maybe you'll find a cracked China teacup of a worry or an old tattered stuffed couch of an ache hiding out in a corner. When you find it, you can say "hello" and even give it a hug. Just like you feel a lot better when someone pays attention to you, listens to what you have to say and accepts you just as you are, these feelings do too.

You're not trying to change or fix anything. The goal is not to get rid of tension in the body and feel better, but that is often a side effect. Once something is seen, heard and accepted, the message has been delivered and it can go away. Imagine if you had an important message to deliver. You knocked on the door, but no one answered. You kept knocking louder and louder…and louder. This is your body. The sooner you listen and receive the message being delivered, the sooner the sensation can go away because its job is done. Just like Jackson's anger. He met it, and he got the message. Then the anger could go away.

Sometimes it feels scary to let in a big emotion. It feels like it may get bigger and bigger and take over. But that's not true. It's like a flower. It starts as a seed, comes into being, lives as a flower for some time and then dissolves back into the earth. Your emotions and sensations have a natural life cycle too.

Body Scan Meet & Greet

"Name It!" is something you can do on the fly. This "Meet & Greet" is more of a full body check in. Do this somewhere cozy without distractions. You can be in any position. I like to do it lying down with a blanket.

Try a quick five-minute version to start your morning stretches, shown in this chapter, or at night as you snuggle into bed. Or anytime you want to listen to your body. Be friendly and curious. Like when there's a new kid at school you want to get to know. Go slow. No need to rush. You can spend five to fifteen minutes doing this.

Have someone read this part to you, (or make a recording for yourself, or check out the online resources for a guided body scan audio):

Pay attention to each part of your body, methodically. Start in your mouth. Notice. Does your tongue feel heavy or thick or tingly? Notice the teeth and your whole mouth. Notice your whole face and whole head. The neck. The left shoulder, arm, hand and each finger – the thumb, pointer finger, middle finger, ring finger and pinky finger. Check out the right side in that same order. Now, the torso – chest, abdomen, back, pelvic bowl. Listen to/ feel into your left leg, knee, calf, ankle and foot. Notice each toe and then pay attention to the other leg in that same order. Notice your whole body. Your whole body as a field of sensation, a palace filled with riches.

That's it! You can grab a piece of paper and some drawing supplies, or your captain's log, and make a map of your palace and what you discovered if you like. You'll find a body map outline in the online resources too. The more you do this Meet & Greet, the more you'll notice.

5 Sense Detective

You experience the world through your five senses. Touch something with your hands, smell it with your nose, see it through your eyes, hear it through your ears and taste with your tongue. This is how you bring the world into you. This is how you are a part of the world – a part of everything. Not feeling a part of everything may be a reason for feeling anxious. Our five senses connect us. They plug us into the world. Pay attention to the way you sense the world for a simple and powerful way to feel more "embodied" – and less anxious.

On the other hand, you may feel overwhelmed with sensory input. Too much noise, weird smells or scratchy sweaters can keep you from feeling calm. When feeling overloaded, go to a quiet space, close your eyes and snuggle under a heavy blanket. It's okay to take a break.

5, 4, 3, 2, 1

You'll learn a lot more about your brain in Chapter 4, and what's happening when you're anxious. The part of your brain that engages with the world through your senses is affected. To re-engage this part of your brain, say out loud five things you can see right now. Say four things you can hear, three things you can touch or feel, two things you can smell and one thing you can taste. Re-engaging your senses can help disengage the anxious response in your brain. It can be helpful to have a friend or other caring person walk you through 5, 4, 3, 2, 1. So be sure others in your life know this tool too.

When feeling anxious, pay close attention to what you feel. If there is a blanket on your lap, get curious about the texture and the weight of it. Notice closely any smells or sounds. Is the room you are in quiet? Do you hear sounds close by or off in the distance? Let the sensations come to you rather than grabbing for them.

~ ~ ~

This is a tool one of Hannah's new friends led her through when she was having a panic attack in the bathroom at school. The decision-making part of Hannah's brain was off-line during this panic. She couldn't think straight. Her friend's logical brain was on and she had learned 5, 4, 3, 2, 1. So she was able to help Hannah.

~ ~ ~

Be a 5 Sense Detective. You can do this anywhere, any time. Have you ever been lying in bed at the end of the day, and you start to panic? Your mind is racing. You worry you forgot something. Or you think about something that happened that day and you're upset it didn't go better. You think about all the scary things happening in the world. And you feel like YOU need to solve these problems. It can feel overwhelming! This is a good time to be a 5 Sense Detective. When you notice what's right here and right now, it takes your mind away from the worry.

Move Your Body

You've learned how to be more aware of your body. Moving your body is another great way to lower anxious feelings. It can also help prevent anxious feelings. Moving your body sends a message to your brain about what's going on around you. When you are frozen in fear, your body sends a danger signal to the brain. Your brain also sends a signal to your body to freeze. It's a two-way street. You can jump in and direct traffic by moving your body and holding it in certain shapes. I'll share many fun ways to do this. Try the ones you like. Start with a few and create your own routine. You'll get some examples of what other kids do too.

~ ~ ~

Olivia was ten years old when she reported feeling anxious every day. It was hard for her to move her body because she was so tense. Olivia started doing some of these stretches each morning before school with her older sister. Her sister was in jr. high school and on the dance team. These stretches helped her get ready for her day, too. Their mom helped them set up a chart so they could mark their progress. Each day they did five minutes of morning stretches, they checked the box for that day. At the beginning, they missed several days each week. They forgot or were running late or had been arguing with each other. On the days they did do it, each one noticed they felt better. Olivia had a little less tension before a quiz in school one day. Her older sister was less sore after dance practice. Each week they recommitted to these five minutes of movement before school. Over time, it became more of a routine. And they both started feeling better. Olivia now could go through a whole day without being overwhelmed by anxiety. This gave her confidence to do more. After a few weeks, Olivia was doing her morning stretches most days. She was able to

40

pay better attention at school and she was also sleeping better. To her, it was totally worth it to make sure she had five minutes every morning to stretch. As a bonus, Olivia and her sister argued less. They were sharing an activity that brought them closer together.

~ ~ ~

Many kids already know that movement can help them feel better. According to a 2005 KidsHealth KidsPoll survey conducted by the National Association of Health Education Centers, children report their main stress in life to be school related. Tests, homework, bullies, peers, and the pressure to attend the "right" schools can contribute to a sense of being overwhelmed. "My family" was the second highest response in that open-ended survey with "brothers/sisters" also mentioned in the top five. Can you relate? When kids were asked what they do when feeling stressed or upset, the number one answer was "play or do something active".

Movement is also a great way to burn off adrenaline that has built up from the stress response. Adrenaline is a hormone (a chemical messenger) that helps your body respond to an emergency. It helps you take action. It floods your system so you quickly get more energy to your muscles and more focus to run away from or fight off a threat. If you don't take action, the adrenaline doesn't get used. Remember the story about spinning fire? That's what happened.

Morning Stretches

Start your day by moving your body. It's too easy to slip out of bed, into the car or bus and into a chair and sit there most of the day. This can contribute to anxious feelings because the body and brain aren't well connected. Wake up your body and brain with a five-minute dance party, a brisk walk with the family dog, jumping on a trampoline or these morning stretches.

"Cow/Cat/Mouse/Dog" begins on the ground. This is the one to do if you're not in the mood to move and want to do just a little something. You can do this by itself or to get ready for "Hello Sun".

If you prefer, start with "Hello Sun". I recommend three rounds. It's amazing the difference you'll feel from the first round to the third round. It takes about three minutes. This series of moves was developed a long time ago by people who were very interested in the mind. This wasn't for physical fitness, though that's a fine side benefit. This was to bring the mind, body and breath together so there's a sense of calm and clarity to take with you into the day.

Here are directions for a variety of tools. Do them all together in this order or just play and have fun picking from these or even make up your own! Finish your morning stretches by sitting or lying on the ground for a minute in quiet. You can go to your Special Place (see Chapter 7) and sit there for a few moments too.

You can do these every morning. Also, as a transition home from school or work. Anytime, really. Best before (not after) a full meal. When I've had it, and it's been a rough day, and I'm about to throw a fit, if I can think of it, moving my body is super helpful. Hopefully a family member can remind you of this helpful tool when you've had it too.

All you need is an open space with a firm surface. Have someone read these directions to you while you do it. I'll share some more ideas for where and when to practice in Chapter 7.

Cow/Cat

This is a simple exercise nearly everyone can do and has wonderful benefit for the spine. It helps it stay flexible and healthy for life while keeping your nervous system strong.

- Begin in a table shape with your hands and knees on the ground.
- Breathe in, lift your chest forward through your arms, look up and "mooooo" like a cow. Keep the lower belly slightly firm.
- Breathe out, relax the tailbone and top of the head toward the floor as you press the middle of your back to the ceiling and pull your belly button up and in towards the spine, like a cat stretching – "meow".
- Repeat this back-and-forth movement several times. Go slow for easy stretching; go faster to feel an increase of energy.

This can also be done sitting in a chair or at the edge of your bed. Reach your heart forward as you breathe in and then curl your back into the letter C as you breathe out. Go back and forth at a pace that feels good to you. Keep your chin level with the ground and rest your hands on your thighs.

Cow/Cat/Mouse/Dog

Let's add two more animals! This is a simple flow that tones and mobilizes the entire spine.

- Breathe in, come into "Cow" (chest up, look up).
- Each time you breathe out, switch between Cat (back rounded) into Mouse (forehead on the floor) on the first one and then Dog (upside down V) on the second one.
- So, it goes like this: Breathe in to Cow, breathe out through Cat into Mouse. Breathe in to Cow, breathe out to Dog. Breathe in to Cow, breathe out through Cat into Mouse. Breathe in to Cow, breathe out to Dog. It can take some time to get the breath and body dancing together so focus on just the body first. The breath will come along for the ride.
- Repeat several rounds and then hold Dog for several rounds of relaxing breaths. In this position, keep your neck relaxed, lift your hips and let your heels sink towards the floor.

Hello Sun

This is my favorite way to start the day. I do this string of stretches three times. It takes five minutes or less. Linking movement and breath organizes and soothes the nervous system while stretching the spine as well as the front and back of the body. The rhythmical movement develops body awareness and coordination. It gets your brain and body ready for the day.

- Start standing strong, like a mountain
- Breathe in and raise both arms out to the sides and up overhead, like you are opening your wings
- Breathe out, fold forward
- Breathe in, place the hands on the shins, and lift the back halfway up like a monkey
- Breathe out, fold again, put your hands on the ground and step back into a push up position, then lower down to the floor – forehead and tops of the feet rest on the floor
- Breathe in, push your hands into the ground and lift your head and chest like a hooded cobra - look up
- Breathe out, to Dog (upside down V)
- Breathe in, jump or step your feet up to your hands and lift the back halfway up like a monkey again

- Breathe out, fold in half and let the top of your head hang towards the ground
- Breathe in, raise both arms up over head like you are opening your wings and come to standing (lead with your heart)
- Breathe out, arms at the sides

Focus on the positions first and then begin to think about coordinating your breath.

Super Star

Your brain takes cues from your body to help figure out what's going on. When you are standing with a strong open posture, your brain takes it as a signal that everything is okay. You are in charge of the situation. Super Star is great to do before you do something that has you feeling nervous or worried.

- Stand with your feet a little bit wider than your hips
- Place your fists on your hips (or straight out at shoulder height)
- Lift your heart and smile – you're a Super Star!
- Hold this position for up to two minutes
- Say positive things to yourself or out loud while being a Super Star, like, "I'm awesome!"

Triangle

Did you know that a triangle is the strongest shape in the universe? Do this posture when you want to feel strong! This is an everyday tool. It has many benefits and is balancing on all levels.

- Step your feet wide.
- Turn your right toes out 90 degrees.
- Lift your left heel, push it away and set it back down (now your left toes are facing a little bit towards the front foot).
- Reach your arms out to the sides at the height of your shoulders, parallel to the ground.
- Extend your right fingertips as if you were trying to reach out over your foot.
- Keep your legs straight and strong, torso long, and then tip to the side until your right hand rests gently on your right shin. No need to try and reach for your foot. Keep your body lined up rather than bending over.

- Reach your left arm up and look to the sky. If you feel tension in your neck, you can look straight ahead or down.
- Expand in all directions. Hold the position steady and strong for five to eight relaxing breaths.
- Reach up to come back up to standing.

~ Switch sides ~

A fun way to switch sides is to turn your feet parallel, jump them together then jump up and turn around. Jump your feet wide and set your feet to repeat the pose on the other side.

Be a Triangle

What parts of your body form the shape of a triangle? Can you find all three? The first one is inside your front arm and front leg. The second is made up of your legs and the floor. The third one is your whole body.

Triangle shapes: Imagine you are the sail on a boat, a rooftop, a witches' hat. What else?

For these next two, you'll balance on one foot. This helps with concentration and focus. It can quiet racing thoughts. The secret to be able to do this is to find something steady across the room to look at. Keep your eyes steady and it will help keep your body steady.

Tree

The tree is a powerful symbol of life. There are many myths about trees. In popular children's tales, trees come to life and are companions to humans. Perhaps it's because trees are our breathing buddies. They breathe in what you breathe out (carbon dioxide) and you breathe in what they breathe out (oxygen). Next time you pass by a tree, take a deep breath in and out and thank the tree for sharing!

- Shift your weight on to one foot.
- Bring your other foot to the inside of the standing leg. The toes of the lifted foot point toward the ground with that bent knee turned out to the side. Put this foot on the calf muscle or thigh muscle – not the knee. It is important to not press the knee sideways.
- Press your foot into your leg and your leg into your foot, keeping your hips centered.
- Begin with your palms pressed together in front of your heart. If you feel steady, carefully reach your arms to the sky.
- Hold steady for several breaths and then switch sides.

Be a Tree

Feel your roots growing into the ground as your arms (branches) grow towards the sun. Wiggle fingers (leaves blowing in the breeze). What kind of tree are you? Oak tree? Cherry tree? Banana tree?

You can "Be a Tree" anytime you want to feel more grounded and connected. When you feel scattered or scared, imagine you have roots growing out through your feet and into the ground. Imagine your roots traveling down past the roots of other trees, down through crystal caves, into the molten core of the earth. Feel this earth energy draw back up into you to feel steady and solid like a tree.

Linda Brody is a certified Anxious to Awesome™ facilitator and a classroom teacher. She starts her mixed grade class with a "Focus Five." Five minutes to help the kids get ready to learn. Good idea, right? The kids in her class get to choose a balance pose to hold for one minute as part of their Focus Five. They often choose Tree.

Bonus Family Activity - Wind in the Trees

I love teaching this in the family classes I teach. Try it at home with your family! (If you can all get together in the same room at the same time – not an easy feat.) It may seem a little goofy, but a good laugh is good medicine. Half the family is trees, the other half is wind. Trees stand steady in Tree pose while the wind blows around the room (run through the trees). Have the trees hold for equal time on each leg. The wind settles down and then... the wind becomes trees and the trees become wind. This helps you practice standing steady and keeping your balance even when things are unsettled around you. It can also help break the tension after a family argument.

Eagle

Eagles are powerful and have incredible vision. Have you ever seen an eagle in the wild?

- Stretch your arms out to the sides at shoulder height to create the enormous wingspan of an eagle.
- Slightly bend your legs then wrap one leg over the top of the other (like you are sitting cross legs on a chair).
- Leave the foot of the top leg on the ground for extra support, like a kick-stand, or lift it slightly off the ground if you are feeling steady. You could even wrap that foot behind the calf of the standing leg.
- Cross your arms in front of your chest past your elbows, bend the elbows and wrap the arms and press the palms together. Or, just bring your forearms closer together if your palms don't reach each other.
- Relax the shoulders and lift the elbows out and up until you feel a fabulous stretch across the "rhomboids" – the muscles between the shoulder blades.
- Anyone who carries around a heavy book/computer bag will appreciate this stretch!
- Hold the pose (using the secret balancing technique) for three to five relaxing breaths. You can deepen this pose by bending your standing leg until your bottom elbow rests on the top thigh.
- Switch sides by unwinding and standing on the other foot. Cross your arms and legs in the opposite direction.

Be an Eagle

Eagles have excellent eyesight. Their eyes allow them to see both forward and to the sides at the same time. Be an eagle and continue to look at just one spot but soften your gaze while in the pose and notice how much you can see above, below and to the sides – without moving your eyes!

Once you've done this on both sides, unwind your arms, open them out to the sides and soar around the room, if you like.

One of the main benefits of this posture is crossing the center of your body. You have two sides to your brain – the emotional brain (the more primitive alarm brain) on the right side and the logical left side. Crossing over the centerline of your body helps the two sides of your brain communicate better. This can help reduce anxious feelings and even panic. Giving yourself a hug or twisting across your body can do the same.

Easy Twist

Twisting is good for your abdominal area and your nervous system. These are two areas of your body that have a lot to do with anxious feelings. Twisting also helps you breathe better. You are about to learn how important this is in the next chapter. Twists massage your digestive organs (and your enteric nervous system, remember that?). They also stretch and massage the diaphragm. This is your major breathing muscle. This simple position also twists your spine which is the main channel for nerves in your body. So simple! So good for you! Twist standing up, sitting in a chair, or on the floor lying down.

- Start with a long, tall spine.
- Turn so your hips and shoulders are towards perpendicular (90 degrees from each other).
- Turn your chin over your back shoulder to complete the twist. If you are lying down, let the ear closest to the floor drop towards the floor.
- Hold the twist for several moments as you breathe slow and easy.
- Then, turn and twist the other way and hold the twist for a bit on this side too.

You'll learn to feel how long to hold a twist and when's the right time to change sides. It should feel gooood!

Tense & Release

Stress and anxious feelings lead to muscle tension. Tense muscles tell the mind there is danger ahead. You can get stuck in this loop of your mind telling your body there is stress and your body telling your mind there is stress. Aak! It's common to hold tension in muscles you are not even aware of, especially when feeling anxious.

This next tool was developed in the 1920s by Dr. Edmund Jacobson to help his patients deal with anxiety. He learned that tensing muscles for a few seconds and then releasing that tension could increase relaxation throughout the whole body. His research showed that it can help with many concerns including low moods, anxiety, panic attacks and racing thoughts. His research showed that doing this also helped people sleep better and have more energy. They also felt calmer and more peaceful. They were able to concentrate better and had higher self-esteem. That's a lot of benefits from such a simple technique!

You need muscle tension to stand and do a million other things. But you don't want to be holding tense muscles when it's not needed. This tool teaches the muscles the difference between tension and relaxation. It increases sensation in the muscles and that increases body awareness. You know we love that!

Dr. Jacobson named it "Progressive Muscle Relaxation." You can call it, "Tense & Release." He wrote a book called, *You Must Relax*. Good advice, right? Here's how.

- Begin lying comfortably on the floor, a couch, your bed…wherever you like.

- Lift just the right leg – only one inch up– and tighten every single muscle in the leg. Squeeze all the muscles in the leg. Squeeze the toes…and release. Let the leg drop.
- Lift the left leg and do the same thing.
- Repeat this throughout all the major muscle groups: lift the hips, squeeze the buttocks, press the low back into the floor, lift the chest and squeeze the shoulder blades, lift each arm, press the neck into the floor, tighten all the muscles in the face…and relax.

Do this:

- At the end of your morning stretches to start a moment of quiet resting
- Before bed to help relax for sleep
- When you get home from school to shed tension from the day
- Anytime you want to wring out stress

You can Tense & Release anywhere in any position. It's nice to do this in a resting position though, because you don't need to use muscle tension to hold your body up. Then, when you release you can really relax.

Ears & Toes Massage

Touching the body increases awareness of it. It's also soothing. Massage or squeeze your arms before a test to feel more focused and present. Rub your arms and legs anytime you want to feel more settled. At home, you can do a sesame oil massage. Sesame oil is very grounding. It's been used in India's health system, Ayurveda, for thousands of years. The oil, the warmth and the massage all calm the nervous system. To do this, use a high-quality organic sesame oil. You only need a few drops.

Do this massage when you're feeling frazzled. It's a wonderful bedtime ritual that can promote deep and restful sleep. This is a primary self-care tool as summer turns to winter. This change of season can make many people feel even more anxious. In northern climates, I recommend doing this at least two to three times a week. Do it every day if you find it helpful.

Simply put a dab of sesame oil on each pointer finger. Rub your thumbs and fingers together to warm up the oil and then massage your outer ears with the warm oil. Start from the top and gently unroll that outer curl. End by massaging and pulling on your ear lobes. This takes about ten seconds. This can be done in the morning right out of the shower to boost mental function and is especially helpful after a loud day.

You can also massage your toes with oil warmed between your fingers. Put on some snuggly socks right after and head to bed for a great night's sleep.

Family Dance Party

Make a morning music playlist. Choose songs that are cheery and make you want to move. Start the day with a family dance party. Choose a theme song for the morning routine. It can be a great way to start the day. Do this instead of or in addition to morning stretches. Do it after school or before dinner if that works better for your schedule.

I'll share my morning playlist with you in the online resources. It includes "Can't Stop the Feeling!" from Trolls soundtrack as well as "Beautiful Day" by U2 and several classic rock tunes, 'cause I'm an old-school rock and roller. What kind of music are you into?

A Day in the Life of Living in Your Body

Here's an example of how, in a few moments, this can fit into your day to feel more embodied and calmer.

- Good morning! Wake up and stretch. Do one or two or a few of the morning stretches.
- Throughout the day. Be a 5 Sense Detective and do mini-body scans – ask yourself "Where do I feel that in my body?" as you engage with the world.
- In the evening. Warm sesame oil ears and toes massage before a bath and Tense & Release when you crawl into bed before sleep.

Start your day with movement. Take a break during the day to move your body. Stretch tense muscles before bed. Your body is home base. It can be a safe haven. Your mind is reflected in your body and your body is reflected in your mind. To take care of your mind, take care of your body.

Captain's Log

Chapter 3 – Breath

"Fear is excitement without the breath."

~ Fritz Perls, MD

D o you sometimes feel like your chest is caving in when you're feeling anxious? Or there's a hollow or vacant feeling there? Maybe your heart is racing. There is a lot going on in the chest. Physically, it's home to your heart and lungs. Energetically, this is your heart center. This is the place where you connect emotionally with the world. This is your "intelligence". Not math and science-wise, but passion and truth and trust.

Let's Get Science-y!

Your breath and nervous system are closely connected. One influences the other. It goes both ways. It's a unique process in your body because it's controlled by the autonomic nervous system (ANS). It can also be under conscious control. Breathing happens without thinking about it (your ANS is in control). You can also jump in at any time and make it happen (your conscious mind is in control). Controlling the breath is one of the best ways to influence your nervous system. Shaping your breath is like having your hand on the control knob of your ANS. This is a *big* secret…the secret key to feeling less anxious and more awesome. We've got a whole chapter dedicated to helping you breathe your best.

Slow, deep breathing is a powerful anti-stress tool. When you bring air down into the lower part of the lungs, where the oxygen exchange is most efficient:

- Heart rate slows

- Blood pressure decreases

- Muscles relax

- Anxiety eases

- The mind calms

This sends a signal to the whole body that there's no emergency and it's okay to chill out.

Watch a baby breathe and you'll see a perfect, natural breath – full, even and rhythmic. It looks like their whole body is breathing. Natural breathing patterns may become restricted or distorted due to chronic stress or trauma. The autonomic nervous system (ANS) then resets itself so this restricted, distorted way of breathing becomes automatic. Yikes! When you're not controlling your breath, you want the breath to be open and unrestricted - naturally. The good news is that practicing these tools for better breathing can help train the ANS to facilitate a healthier breath when it is running on autopilot. Sweet!

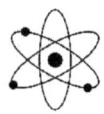

Better Breathing Habits

Anxious feelings can take your breath away, and not in a good way. Your breath is something you can manage. Shaping your breath directly affects the nervous system. The nervous system controls stress and anxious feelings. Change your breath and you can change your nervous system. It's like learning to control the dials on the Stress-O-Meter. You can turn the stress down with longer, slower breathing.

You can exercise your breathing system. It's like taking your breath to the gym to get more fit. You know now that this also helps your brain and whole nervous system to be more fit too. Your autonomic nervous system (ANS) develops a set point. It currently may be set to "anxious". You can change this set point with better breathing habits. Practice these breathing tools every day to improve your natural breathing habits. You can also do them when you start to feel anxious. It will be easier if you're already used to doing them, so they are comfortable and familiar. Breathe well to live well.

Crocodile Breath

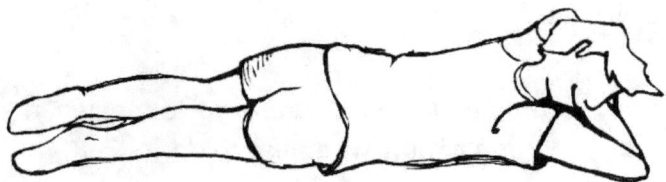

It's common to hold a lot of tension in the belly. This makes it harder to take a full breath. Have you ever had someone say to you, "take a deep breath" and you find that you can't? Tension in the tummy (abdomen) may be one reason. Not understanding how your breath works may be another. Crocodile Breath uses the floor so your whole belly gets feedback and can relax.

To be a Crocodile, lie on your belly. Stack one hand on top of the other and turn your head to rest one cheek on your stacked hands. Let your big toes touch and your heels fall away from center. As you breathe in, feel your whole belly spread out on the floor. As you breathe out, feel your whole body sink into the floor. Do this for a few minutes. After a few breaths, turn your head and rest the opposite cheek on the stacked hands. Focus on breathing out longer and slower than you breathe in. It's soothing and quieting. You're training your abdomen to relax and allow a full breath. This turns on the "rest and digest" side of your nervous system. And speaking of digesting, this is best done when you don't have a full stomach.

Crocodile is a great way to begin & end the body practices in Chapter 2. You can also do this one thing in the morning to start your day. You can do it when you get home from school. You can do it when your brother or sister is bothering you and you'd rather relax your breath than get in trouble. And, this will feel wonderful at the end of the day before bed. It's best done on a firm surface. A carpeted floor, yoga mat or pad or a stack of blankets on a wood floor is ideal. Your bed is too squishy. Once you know Crocodile Breath, you can do it sitting up anywhere by placing your hand on your abdomen.

This is my recommended number one go-to tool when you don't know what else to do.

This is my recommended number one go-to tool when you don't know what else to do. You are learning lots of tools to lessen and even prevent anxious feelings. But it's easy to feel overwhelmed and then it's hard to choose. Mark this one in the book or write the word "Crocodile" on a sticky note and put it by your bed. That's all you have to do.

Buddy Breathing

Here's another way to invite deeper breathing. Place a stuffed bean toy on your belly to help slow and deepen the breath. The physical weight of the toy helps you breathe out more. Feeling the toy on your belly brings more awareness to breathing. Lie on your back and place a small stuffed animal on the belly, between the lower ribs and hips. Imagine you're giving this stuffed friend a ride on the ocean wave of breath. It is not done with effort, but with relaxed awareness. Like a nice vacation day at the beach. Sun is shining. Warm sand. Light breeze. Clear blue sky. Buddy Breathing signals the nervous system to trigger the relaxation response too.

Balloon Breath

I love this one! It's so silly and fun. Body and breath move together in a very basic and obvious way. As you stand up and reach up, the physical movement helps your body take a breath in. When you flop to the ground, it helps your body release the breath. Plus, it just feels good to flop your body on the floor.

- Squat on the floor. You are a balloon! Hug your knees and squeeze all the air out of your balloon.

- Inhale to inflate. Breathe in as you stand up and stretch up, bringing your hands all the way up over your head, filling your balloon with air.

- Let all the air out. Breathe out as you flutter to the ground like a balloon losing air until you are lying on the floor.

Let's do it again! What color balloon are you? Squat down and squeeze all the air out, and then imagine the color of your balloon as you breathe in and stand up to inflate. Breathe out fluttering to the ground. This one is worth repeating a few times. After the last round, lie on the ground and rest.

Have you ever felt like flopping to the ground in despair or frustration? Do this then. This is also a great morning activity or as a transition home from school. Do it in an area with room to flutter and flop without bumping into anything (or anyone).

Don't be surprised if you come home from school and find your mom or dad flopped on the boldly patterned living room rug like a deflated balloon. They also need these tools because grown-ups get anxious too!

Breathing Wings

Like Balloon Breath, this physical movement guides the breath. When it feels hard to "take a deep breath", moving your arms like this can help. Reaching the arms out and up stretches the muscles between the ribs (the intercostal muscles) and pulls the lungs open, inviting in a deeper breath. Also, matching breath with movement soothes the nervous system.

- Stand in an open space
- Breathe in and sweep your arms straight out to the sides and up as if you're opening your majestic wings
- Breathe out and slowly lower them down at your sides
- Open your wings several times

To get your breath and body to move together may be hard at first. Focus only on the movement. Your breath will follow along.

What kind of bird are you? Imagine the color, shape and texture of your wings. This can also be done sitting (or even flying around the room). Start your morning stretches with Breathing Wings or anytime you want your chest to feel more open and freer. Do it inside, outside, anywhere you like. Next time you are stressed-out, run around outside with your Breathing Wings. Who cares what the neighbors think.

Breathe Out More

Crocodiles, Balloons and Breathing Wings, oh my! You're using your body to breathe better with all these tools.

A study published in the May 2019 International Journal of Psychophysiology reported on the effects of slower and longer breathing on decision-making. Study participants did two minutes of either a) deep even breathing, or b) breathing out twice as long as they breathed in. Just two minutes! Then the participants did "a 30-minute business challenging decision-making task with multiple choice answers." The participants in this study reported feeling less stressed. They also got 50% more questions right than another group who did not do any specific breathing before the task. The results of this study showed that two minutes of either of this kind of full breathing led to feeling less stress and being more focused.

Do you realize what this means? Two minutes of relaxed slow and long breathing before a test or assignment can help you feel calmer and get a better score. Yay! You can totally do this. Don't give up if it doesn't work right away. It may take some practice. Stick with it.

Remember in the first chapter where you learned about the two sides of the autonomic nervous system (ANS)? One is the stress side (sympathetic) and the other is the rest side (parasympathetic). Breathing in is a sympathetic function. It alerts and energizes. Breathing out is a parasympathetic function. It quiets and calms. Your resting rhythm is ideally one to two breathing. That means you breathe out twice as long as you breathe in. This is a good breathing habit to develop. Then, when you're not thinking about your breath, or shaping it in any way, it falls into this healthy, natural rhythm. This becomes your nervous system's new set point for calm.

> *This becomes your nervous system's new set point for calm.*

So what exactly does this look like? Here is a step-by-step. Have someone read this to you while you do it.

- Sit or stand in a tall, relaxed position. Like a noble king or queen sitting on the throne - not hunched over, not tense.
- Pay attention to your breath
- Count the breath*
- Slowly and gently start to guide your breath into a pattern**
- Repeat this pattern as long as it feels comfortable to you. Do this with no effort or strain. Set a timer for two to five minutes. Or count five cycles of breath (in + out = one cycle).

*To count seconds, as kids we said "one Mississippi, two Mississippi, three Mississippi...". Maybe because I grew up in the Twin Cities in Minnesota, the first major cities on the river we call, the "Mighty Miss". It takes a second to say, "Mississippi". Choose your own word. You could say "one peace, two peace..." These days, I like to use the word "OM". It's a nice full, one beat sound. I'll use this one as an example. Breathe in and repeat in your mind, "OM one, OM two, OM three, OM four". Breathe out and mentally say, "OM one, OM two, OM three, OM four, OM five, OM six, OM seven, OM eight."

**The pattern is to breathe in for four seconds and breathe out for six to eight seconds. Work your way towards it.

The Great Pause

This guidebook is for families who are beginning to look into more holistic ways to be well. It's a beginner's book. And yet…I wouldn't feel right if I didn't introduce this very special breathing tool – holding your breath. The truth is, at first it may cause more anxious feelings. Try this after you feel comfortable with other tools in this book and have a good habit of moving your body and breath. The benefits are so great, it's worth looking into. When someone is anxious, they tend to hold their breath or breathe very shallow. When you try to hold your breath, right away it can trigger some panic. So, if you start when you are relaxed and you are moving your breath around anyway, it can be much easier.

Practice The Great Pause when you are not feeling anxious. It helps strengthen your breathing system and creates a less anxious state overall. The diaphragm is a big dome-like sheet of muscle at the base of your lungs. It's the main muscle used in breathing. Holding your breath puts pressure on this muscle and makes it stronger. It's like Tense & Release for your diaphragm. Muscles in your body are likely tense when you're anxious. The diaphragm can also be tight from short, shallow breathing. Holding your breath is like taking your breathing muscles to the gym for a workout. It will make you stronger, help you breathe better and help you feel less anxious.

A person can hold their breath for about 30 seconds on average. Someone who practices holding their breath on a regular basis can comfortably hold their breath for one minute…or more. When anxious feelings are present, you may not be able to hold your breath at all. This is why you'll want to try this when you are feeling calm.

You can think about The Great Pause as swimming in a cold mountain lake. You dip your toe in and "oooh!" you pull it right back out. Hold your breath for two seconds. Then, you try it again and maybe this time you don't pull it out so quickly. This time, hold for five seconds. Slowly, over time, you acclimate and get used to the cold water. Holding your breath for 10, 20 or even 30 seconds. Eventually you can plunge your whole body in and it feels A H H M A Z I N G.

When I was a kid, I loved to swim. I still do! One of my favorite things to do was to throw a hair clip or coin into the deep end of the pool and dive for it. My friends and I would swim hard down to the bottom of a 13-foot-deep diving pit, have a "tea party" where we pretended to eat two cookies and drink a cup of tea as fast as we could and then shoot back up to the surface. Who knew it was so good for our health?

One of my favorite sayings is, "When you find yourself in a paradox, you know you are approaching the truth." A paradox means something seems true and false at the same time. In this case, holding your breath. Good or bad? Not so good when you do it habitually because you feel anxious. Good when you do it as an exercise, like lifting weights, to develop better breathing habits and gain all the benefits. The main difference is if you are doing it with awareness or not.

Here's my suggestion. Sneak up on the pause. Breathe in and then hold your breath for one second and let it go. Notice how you feel. Do that whenever you are feeling brave, calm, adventurous.

Throughout the day, notice if you're holding your breath. It's common with people who feel anxious. When you do notice, let it go and take a few relaxing breaths. You'll get the hang of it. Here's another way to say it. Holding breath with awareness = strengthening the Great Pause...keep at it. Holding breath when anxious = signal to relax with a few deep even breaths.

This is important. You can do this. I believe in you. Take your breath to the gym with these breathing tools, every day, and then let it flow the rest of the day.

Square Breath

There are four parts to a square and four parts to your breath. Use your finger to trace a square in the air to match each of the 4 "sides" of your breath. Trace your finger up one side of the invisible square as you breathe in. Trace your finger across the top of the square as you hold your breath. Trace your finger down the other side of the square as you breathe out. Trace your finger across the bottom of the square as you hold your breath again. Breathe in and start a second round of square breathing. Try this two, three or four rounds.

Square Breath helps you play with The Great Pause. Another benefit of holding your breath is that it can quiet your mind.

~ ~ ~

Remember Olivia from the last chapter? Before she learned these tools, she had headaches and stomachaches in the morning. This led to several missed days of school. She didn't make the connection that the aches she had were from the stress of tests and homework. At her first class with me, Olivia reported feeling stressed "every day." She learned Crocodile Breath and also enjoyed Balloon Breath. After learning these breathing tools, Olivia had an "aha" moment that she could breathe out more. She realized that this is something she could do before a test. She started to develop a toolbox of effective tools to help her manage anxious feelings.

~ ~ ~

It's in Your Hands

This next set of tools could be the most helpful set of tools you learn in this book. Of all the tools I teach kids to manage anxious feelings, these are the most popular. They're really special. In the last chapter, you learned certain positions like Triangle and Tree. These tools are positions for your hands. They are called Mudras, which sounds like moo-draa.

Your breath regulates your nervous system and it also influences your energy body. What is your energy body? It's the non-physical part of you. You can't see it or hear it or smell it, but you can feel it. And you can feel its effect in your everyday life.

One of the reasons you feel anxious could be because you are a sensitive person. You're more aware of the subtle realms (the energy that is in and around you), and you can feel other people's emotions. This can be overwhelming. But when you practice the Body tools in Chapter 2, along with these breathing exercises and hand gestures in this chapter, you'll be able to manage and direct this sensitivity. It's a valuable asset!

You won't hear your doctor talking about your energy body because it's something modern medicine doesn't study. Scientists in different fields have been studying the human energy body for a long time. It's a part of our everyday language. The term "good vibes" refers to a person's energy.

Mudras balance your energy and develop awareness. Each one has its own flavor and you will experience it in your own unique way. They can help you quickly feel calm, confident and centered. They can also cultivate a strong and clear mind. They can help you feel more connected and aware. Make notes in your captain's log of what you felt during your mudra practice and how you feel after. Practice just one at a time or several in a row. This can help you compare them and choose which one feels right for you at which times.

~ ~ ~

I teach these tools to many groups of children. One class I taught was in the lunchroom after school. One day, I taught the kids a mudra called "Turtle in a Shell." (Described below) Riley was in this class. I hadn't yet given an explanation of how it works or what the benefits were. As soon as she put her hands into this shape, she proclaimed, "Oh, this makes me feel so stable and strong." This girl was harassed daily by a boy at school. She went on, "I know! I'm going to use this mudra when that boy is bothering me so I can feel this way instead of the way I usually feel when he is bugging me." The next week in class, we started with a check-in. I asked the kids how they had been using these tools to feel less anxious. Riley said, "I use this mudra all the time (showing Turtle in a Shell). I taught my sister, and she uses it all the time. I taught my best friend, and she uses it all the time now, too." You too can use these simple hand gestures to shift your mental state.

~ ~ ~

Mudras are a wonderful tool for a quick reset during the day.

Mudras are a wonderful tool for a quick reset during the day. These are great before a test or any situation when you want to be focused and open. They are also a great way to start a moment of silent sitting. You can also literally whip these out of your pockets and do them on the train, at your desk, while standing in line, on the couch or in your Special Place.

To do them:

- Find a comfortable seated position
- Sit tall with the crown of your head over the base of your spine
- Relax the whole body
- Place your hands into one of the positions described below and sit for several moments

Notice:

- Sensations in your body
- How and where your breath is moving in your body
- The quality of thoughts in your mind (is your mind busy or quiet?)

Turtle in a Shell

Fold thumbs into palms and wrap fingers around them making loose fists with thumbs tucked inside. Sometimes I say, "Put the hot dog (your thumb) into the hot dog bun (your wrapped fingers)." Place hands on thighs, palms down. This mudra may help reduce feelings of anxiety and instill a sense of stability and calm. It can feel cooling and quieting. How does it feel for you?

Plug into the Earth

Hold your hands up and make "peace signs" with your first two fingers pointing up. Ring and pinky fingers held down by thumbs. Turn hands down and plug those first two fingers on each hand into the earth by pressing the tips into the floor at your side. This mudra can be grounding and stabilizing. What do you think?

Whole World

Bring the tips of each one of your fingers on one hand to touch that same fingertip of the other hand. The palms open out away from each other. Like you're holding the whole world in your hands. This may be helpful for improving overall energy level and expanding awareness in all directions. What do you notice?

~ ~ ~

Liza is a 5th grader who uses Whole World mudra every day in school. She can do it at her desk without anyone knowing. It calms her down when she's having a hard time with friends.

She taught this to her friend in the bathroom one day when she was having a hard time too. Her friend felt better right away.

~ ~ ~

Heart Flower

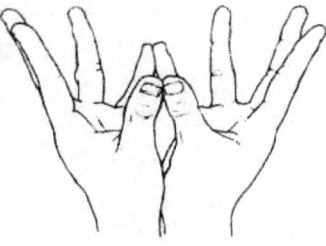

Bring palms together at your heart. Keep the base of the palms, pinky fingers and thumbs touching. Then spread your middle fingers out away from center, like a flower blooming. Imagine your flower opening and sense that opening in your heart. Open to receive grace, an insight, love. What does your heart flower smell like? What color is it? Where and when would you like to have this feeling again?

I worked with a 12-year-old boy named Sam who was unable to move his hands into these shapes on his own. I helped him shape his hands and held them in place with my hands so he could feel them for himself. If your hands work differently, you can still do these hand shapes. Have someone help hold your hands into the position or imagine/visualize your hands in the shape – you'll still experience the benefits!

Your breath and your hands are something you always have with you. Use these tools every day to manage your anxious feelings and prepare your nervous system to be more stress-hardy.

Captain's Log

Chapter 4 – Mind

"If the mind is strong, anything can be achieved."

~ Swami Satchidananda

Where to begin? The mind is incredible. It's awesome. As I've shared, people from various parts of the world have been studying the mind in depth for thousands of years. By paying very careful attention, they came to understand what modern science has only recently been able to measure. They also had a lifestyle of being connected to their own body and breath as well as the world around them.

The brain is the mechanism for the mind. Very little was understood about the brain until new imaging techniques were developed that allowed us to see brain activity. Since this time, understanding of the brain has exploded (um, gross, I didn't mean it like that). This ancient wisdom is something modern imaging technology can now verify. You too can become a master of your own mind. Science proves it.

> *Brain imaging technology, called fMRI, was first developed in 1977 and came into more common use in the 1990s. fMRIs measure changes in blood flow in the brain that indicates activity.*

Your mind is like the internet – it's everywhere. Your brain is like the phone in your hand – it's the device you use to interact with the mind.

A laser is so powerful because all that energy is focused into a single beam. When that light is scattered, it's not as effective. Your mind is like this too. You're probably familiar with scattered thoughts. It can be hard to pay attention. In this chapter I'll share everyday tools to collect and focus the powerful energy of your mind. You'll also learn to quiet racing thoughts. Plus, you'll learn to better understand your mind and use it to live a beautiful life. As with the other chapters, pick and choose what feels right for you. Come back later and dive in for more. This is a big chapter because we are talking about the mind and the brain. Big stuff.

Baseball

Okay, who loves baseball? I do! I spent time each summer of my childhood on my grandparent's farm in Iowa. One of the background sounds to my time on the farm was afternoon Cubs baseball games crackling on the AM radio. My grandma was a big Cubs fan! I've created a big, plowed neural highway in my brain for baseball (more on this in a moment). So, I sometimes like to use baseball to explain the brain and the mind.

Your brain is like a pitching machine. Instead of pitching out a five-ounce, nine-inch, white leather ball with 108 red stitches, your brain pitches thoughts:

- Positive thoughts
- Negative thoughts
- Happy and sad thoughts
- Thoughts about the past and the future

It also pitches beliefs, your personality and your sense of self. A belief is a thought you keep repeating. If you keep thinking something negative about yourself – or someone else – over and over, you'll start to believe it is true. It's the same thing for positive thoughts.

It's not possible to count each thought, but scientists have tried! The National Science Foundation researched how many thoughts the average person has in a day. They did this by following what they call "thought worms". It's estimated that a person has about 60,000 a day! Turns out, a lot of them are negative (80%) and almost all of them (95%) are repetitive – the same thoughts you had the day before, and the day before that and the day before that. Sheesh! The mind is super complex, and this is a tiny peek into what may actually be happening in the mind, but it helps you understand that:

- The mind produces a ginormous number of thoughts
- The majority of these thoughts are worry-type thoughts
- Of these many thoughts, most of them are the same thoughts over and over

What does this tell us? That your mind is trying to keep you safe! It's looking out for danger (what's wrong = negative thoughts) and finding safety in sameness (repetitive thoughts).

Negative thoughts include worry, criticism, complaining and resisting (like, "I don't want this"). Racing thoughts and anxious feelings go together so there can be even more thoughts in a day when in this state.

But guess what? Scientists at Cornell University found that 85% of what we worry about never happens. This was self-reported by the participants of the study. Of the 15% of the worries that did happen, 79% of the subjects in this study found that they could handle the challenge better than they expected. Or they learned something worthwhile while facing the challenge. This is good news. Now you know that your worries only have about a 15% chance of turning into something. AND, if they do, you can handle it and even grow from it.

Repetitive thoughts create your reality. It's the story of "me". It's common to think the same things over and over and this becomes who you are. You can choose your thoughts to become who you want to be. You can direct these thoughts. You can shape them and sculpt who you are. The tools in this book help you manage your mind.

The mind in this baseball example is the power that runs the pitching machine. The mind does the thinking, feeling and choosing. None of this works without the brain. The brain is the machine, and the mind is the operator of the machine.

As you develop your mind, you get to choose if you are the batter at bat, responding to the pitch (your thoughts). Or sitting in the stands watching each pitch. This is like meditating. I'll teach you how to meditate in this chapter. Ooh! There goes a slider. Wow! A fastball. Ooops, a foul. You're not rooting for either team, you're simply interested in watching the pitch.

Then, because you've learned so much about the different kinds of pitches your mind generates through the pitching machine of your brain, you'll become a slugger. When you're having a great day, it's like you're batting 1,000. You're responding to your thoughts with skill and grace. You won't swing at the foul balls (negative thoughts). And you can hit it out of the park with the perfect pitch of a positive thought. That's what the tools in this chapter are for.

Many kids I work with feel anxious when things aren't just right. They struggle with perfectionism. They have unrealistic expectations and put a lot of pressure on themselves.

~ ~ ~

This was the case with Santiago. His dad was a Chicago police officer. The work of a first responder can be stressful and dangerous. Santiago had wonderful, supportive parents who helped him put his dad's work into perspective, but it still made him feel anxious. As one way to deal with this, Santiago worked very hard to get the highest scores in school and on the field. When he did do well, which was most of the time, he struggled to enjoy his accomplishments. He was a Cubs fan too. Aramis Ramirez was his favorite player. At the time, Ramirez was one of the best hitters on the team and his batting average was about .300. That means he hit 30% of the balls pitched to him. The best hitter of all-time in Major League Baseball is Ty Cobb. His batting average is .366. That's an average of 36%. The very best ever! This is something Santiago and I talked about a lot. It was a helpful perspective to see that you can be the very best at something and be nowhere near 100%.

~   ~   ~

Nobody bats 1,000. It's just a saying. Do you struggle with perfectionism? How does it feel when things don't go just right? Make some notes in your captain's log.

You can use the tools in this book to manage your thoughts and feelings about being perfect. It's okay to excel. It's fantastic to strive to be your best, but not if it over-runs your life with anxious feelings.

In this chapter, we'll also explore the three parts of your brain, your brain's filtering system and a network that gets active when your brain is relaxed. And we'll check out what's happening in these areas when you're anxious. Then, we'll take a closer look at the mind. Of course, there will be tools and activities to help too. If this seems interesting to you, let's Get Science-y! Otherwise, feel free to skim through or skip past to the tools at the end of the chapter.

Let's Get Science-y!

This is going to be the most mega-science-y section of this book. The mind and brain are incredibly complex and fascinating. You are the captain of this ship (your mind and body) and the better you understand it, the more you can operate it with skill. We know so much more today

86

than a few short decades ago. When you're an adult, we'll know even more.

You are the captain of this ship (your mind and body) and the better you understand it, the more you can operate it with skill.

Perhaps you'll become an explorer in this emerging field of science. Deep sea exploration began in the late 1800's. Outer space exploration took off in the 1960s. Brain and mind science is happening right now. Mirror neurons were first measured in monkeys in 1991. Scientists are still not sure of their purpose. They have something to do with how we relate to others. The modern field of neuroscience and human psychology is in its infancy. You may be the one to make the next major discovery of the intricate workings of the mind.

3 Brains in 1

Let's start with the brain. It weighs about three pounds in an average adult. It makes up 2% of the total body and uses 20% of the oxygen supply. It is made up of more than 70% water. It has as many neurons (brain cells) as there are stars in the Milky Way galaxy – about 100 billion. There are many parts to your brain. Let's look at the areas that have to do with how much anxiety you experience and how you respond to anxious feelings. You're also going to learn simple tools to help your brain be its best.

There are three major areas of function in the brain. The oldest part is called the reptilian brain. It's like a robot. It receives programming and then operates that program without emotion or conscious thought. This part of your brain has one job – to keep you alive. Your brain is hard-wired to keep you safe. This is where the stress response alarm goes off.

It happens without thinking. This is the instinctive brain. At this primitive level, change is dangerous. Sameness is safe. This is one reason it's hard to start a new habit or change a behavior. And why new situations may create anxiety.

Back in the cave-people days, if you went out of your cave, turned right, found some berries and made it back to the cave safely, that action got wired into the brain. It was easy to go that route. If you went out of the cave and turned left, you would get a panicky feeling. Your mind would worry. That route is not known and so, not safe at this primitive level. This is one reason why routine can help you feel calm and nurtured today.

The second part is the emotional brain, the limbic system. You could call this your monkey mind. This is the area of everyday thoughts, preferences, and emotions. This part of your brain loves novelty (new and different things), and this is why you get distracted. It responds to feelings.

The amygdala is an almond-shaped area within the emotional center of your brain. It perceives a threat (from within or without) and your whole body responds. Some people who have anxiety may have an overactive or hyper-sensitive amygdala. Everyday situations may feel threatening and could set off the alarm in your brain. It's like the alarm is too sensitive or there may be a false alarm. You can soothe this part of your brain by being in nature, doodling, daydreaming or connecting with people you care about.

The third part of your brain that developed most recently in humans (but still millions of years ago) is the pre-frontal cortex. This is the fancy, modern part of your brain. It controls rational thought and a whole lotta complex behaviors, planning skills and even your personality. This is what separates humans from all other animals. This is your wise, rational self. This is where you can consider other viewpoints, solve a problem and think about the future. This is the area that allows you to choose how to respond to the alarm set off in another part of the brain. You can call this your wise brain. And, just a note, it's not fully developed until you're in your mid-20s. The tools in this guidebook support this development.

When you're under duress or have a strong emotional experience like anger or anxiety, your wise brain isn't fully functioning. All the energy used for math equations, language learning and problem solving is redirected to the emergency. Here again, your brain is being energy efficient. This "emergency" can be any kind of an alarm, like a worry about why your mom isn't home from work yet. This is why it can feel impossible to do your homework when you're worried. And why your wise brain can't always reason its way out of anxiety. This is also why anxious feelings can build up to a full panic and really disrupt your life.

This is why it can feel impossible to do your homework when you're worried.

This part of the brain is coaxed back online after an alarm through activities like talking it out, reading or writing. You could even run through some math problems if that's your thing!

~ ~ ~

This worked well for Devon, a six-year-old in one of my classes. He has an Autism Spectrum Disorder (ASD). Devon would get overwhelmed by what was going on in class – the lights, the sounds, the schedule. Guess what calmed him down? Reading a book! I kept a stack of picture books in class. When he started running around, flapping his hands and squealing, I would grab a book, run over and hand it to him. He immediately would sit down and begin reading. He was an excellent reader. The reason this helped him is because it engaged his wise brain and brought him out of a state of alarm and overwhelm.

~ ~ ~

The robot brain wants safety and routine. The monkey brain wants art and friends. It wants to play and discover new things. The wise brain wants to solve puzzles, analyze, read a book (like Devon did) or talk about what's going on.

Of course, the brain is wildly more complex than this. But it can be helpful to consider if your brain is focused more on safety, creativity or logic. It can be all at once, but one is typically more active. Anxiety is part of the safety features of your brain. When you can see this for yourself, you can soothe yourself by taking care of the robot, the monkey and the wise parts of your brain with the activities that make them happy – routine and familiarity, connection and creativity or logic and reasoning.

The tools you are learning throughout this book can help calm and soothe these three areas in your brain so they operate at their best.

Brain Filter and Blue Butterflies

There are a gazillion things flying at your brain every moment. You can't possibly take in and manage it all, so your brain sets up a filtering system based on your preferences and beliefs. You get to set this filter. You are the captain! This area is called the reticular activating system (RAS). When you go to a buffet, you don't eat all the food on display. You choose what you like and leave the rest. That's what the RAS does for filtering and sorting the gazillion things flying at your brain. You're creating your own reality. Not a lot gets in. This is your brain's spam filter.

> *You're creating your own reality. Not a lot gets in. This is your brain's spam filter.*

RAS is like a guard at the door. It chooses who gets in, based on your settings. The settings are created based on emotion. When you are super excited about something, your brain interprets this as important and sets a filter to look for it again. When you are super worried or scared about something, your brain interprets it as important and sets a filter to look for it again too.

> *"The brain takes its shape from what the mind rests upon."*
>
> ~ *Rick Hanson, Ph.D.*

You see what you believe. This is called confirmation bias. It means your brain is looking for things you have filtered for. You may have heard the saying, "I'll believe it when I see it." But what's really happening is that you are seeing it *because* you believe it. Let's put it all together. Repetitive and negative thoughts are kind of like your brain's filtering program to keep you safe. It's looking for what's wrong so you can stay away from it. Being the captain of your ship means that you are also programming for awesome stuff. You're teaching your brain to look for what's right so you'll experience more of that.

Let's test this out. Let's set a filter for blue butterflies. You probably don't feel any strong emotion about them either way so it's a good subject for practice. Think about blue butterflies and generate some positive feelings for them. I like to call it "game show feelings". Like, when a contestant on a game show is jumping up and down, squealing with delight and clapping their hands while a big colorful wheel spins before it lands on the prize. Notice the feeling in your body. Yay! Blue butterflies! Now, your brain has interpreted all this as something important. You have thoughts and emotions around blue butterflies, so your brain sets a filter for it. NOW, in the next 48 hours, you will very likely see a blue butterfly. It could be an actual butterfly, or it could be on a teacup, or someone's T-shirt. It could be a decal in a window or an emoji in a text. Fun, right? Start with easy stuff that you don't have a strong desire or aversion for. Then, with practice, you can continue to set your brain's filter in this way with things that matter more to you.

This guard (the RAS filter) also has another job working the 3rd shift at the factory making sure all the automation (your habits) runs smoothly. A new habit is learned in the wise brain and then it gets moved to this part of your brain factory. Remember when you first tried to tie a pair of shoes? I do. It was a sunny afternoon in early June. My sister ran off to play with friends and I wasn't allowed to go until I tied my own shoes. I was so frustrated! I was also motivated to get out there and play. I put one knee down on the linoleum kitchen floor as the June breeze beckoned through the red screen door. I had to pay very close attention as I worked with the long, soft cotton laces. It was hard to get the loops to go the way they needed to. Plus, I hadn't learned the pattern for making the tie. Now, I can tie my shoes "without thinking" about it while doing something else at the same time. This same process happens with all our habits. Walking, riding a bike and playing a musical instrument all require intense concentration to learn at first and then become a habit. It starts in the fancy, modern part of your brain as you are learning and then gets moved to the automation area of the brain. This saves a lot of brain power.

Now you understand why trying something new feels hard. It's like whacking through a dense jungle. Then over time, it becomes a high-speed well-traveled highway. These highways are called "neural connections". Like the neural highway in my brain for baseball. This is a habit. Repeated thoughts, beliefs and activities plow the road more and more. These become ruts in the road. Wanted and unwanted. You can create a highway of fear and it becomes hard to pull out of that rut. You can also plow a highway of joy. Through repetition it's easier for your brain to stay in that groove. You'll be in the express lane of good feelings. Kids have an advantage because they don't have as many well-plowed roads as adults do.

Daydreams and the Default Mode Network

Not too long ago, scientists discovered areas of the brain that are more active when at rest than when engaged in focused activity. This is very cool and somewhat mysterious because when you think of the brain like a computer or a machine, the on-task activities would require more power than at-rest activities.

On task is like tying your shoes. Off task is like staring out the window. While staring out the window, your mind is wandering through a garden of thoughts that include:

- Remembering the past
- Thinking about yourself and others
- Loose, random thoughts
- Appreciating the way the leaves on the tree outside flutter in the breeze

This is called daydreaming and something I often got in trouble for in school, even though it turns out that it benefits my brain.

It seems that when the brain is at rest there's something important happening. It could be the brain filing things away or repairing itself or laying down new networks. It's okay to take a break. It helps your brain.

It's okay to take a break. It helps your brain.

Do you know what doesn't work when you're daydreaming? Your brain's filtering system, the RAS. This is why you often get a great insight or creative idea in this state. The guards at this gate are on break and all kinds of unusual things can get in. Isn't the brain so cool?

When someone shouts, "Eureka!" this is what just happened.

Two great scientists, Albert Einstein and Thomas Edison – napped for insight. They wanted to catch the curious ideas that could sneak in past the RAS guard at the door as they drifted off to sleep.

Now that you understand the mechanics of your brain a little better, let's look into the mind more.

Mindfulness

You've probably heard this word. You may have practiced mindfulness at school. You choose something to shine the flashlight of your awareness on – your breath, a flower or thoughts in the mind. The goal is to pay attention.

There are hundreds of ways to do this. And you can do it with anything. You can pay careful attention while you eat dinner or watch the sunset. You can pay attention to your footfalls as you wander through a forest. You can pay attention to the endless circle of your breath.

Meditation helps your mind be more peaceful.

Meditation, a mindfulness tool, helps your mind be more peaceful. Some studies have shown that meditation may reduce the activity of an overactive part of your brain (the amygdala), lowering anxious feelings. It can help you be less reactive.

Another word for mindfulness is awareness. See where we're going here? It's not a matter of trying to fix or change yourself or anything in the world. You can learn to be a keen observer. Rather than getting into a fistfight with the day, step out of the ring and watch. Watch your mind, watch how your body reacts, watch what's happening around you. This can help with anxiety.

I often find myself wrestling with what is. I want things to be different! A little more of this, or less of that. I may find myself disagreeing with the weather or the long line to check out at the grocery store. I can't change the weather outside, but I can change the weather inside.

You can befriend anxious feelings. You're changing your relationship to things and people and places. You can have anxious feelings and still be awesome.

From this place of awareness, you can access a deep knowing. I like to call it your "inner wisdom". This wisdom is always guiding you, but there may be too much chatter, too much static on the line to receive it. Meditation clears the static and gets you in the habit of paying attention to this guidance. From here you will be guided to right action. This is freedom.

Mental Hygiene

Please raise your hand if you brush your teeth. Keep your hand raised if you brush your teeth at least twice a day. Okay, I can't see you, but I bet your hand is raised. Why do you brush your teeth? Depending on your age, you may say, "My mom makes me." Good. Why does she make you? Answers I've heard include, "It keeps my teeth healthy." and "It feels good." or, "It feels gross if I don't." Many of you even floss. This is called dental hygiene. You do it every day, and maybe even twice a day. It takes about two minutes and it's a habit for life. When you're running late, you still brush your teeth. When you're in a bad mood, you still brush your teeth. You take care of your teeth. No big deal.

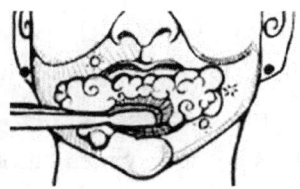

Let's do the same for our mind. Let's take care of it. Two minutes a day, twice a day, practice mental hygiene as well as dental hygiene. You can even stack them and do them at the same time. Brush your teeth and then sit quietly for two minutes.

It can seem kinda boring at first and maybe even not that helpful, but I promise that in a few years, you'll be so glad you have this daily habit. In ten years, your life will be very different than it would have been if you never did this. I've been practicing mental hygiene for several decades now. It didn't seem like it made that much of a difference but, looking back, I see it's had a profound effect on my sense of self, my level of satisfaction and peace, and my mental health.

That two minutes makes you feel better right away too. So, you get the benefits of the single time you do it, and the benefits of doing it consistently over time.

You don't need to be successful at it right away. You can sit quietly with your mind jumping around like a monkey the whole time and you still benefit. Cool, right? You're learning to be with what is. Your mind's job is to think. Thank you, mind! Thoughts arise. And you practice noticing. "Ah, ha" you say. "I'm thinking about that math test." Or, "I'm hungry." Or, you're thinking about how to get to the next level in your video game. That's fine. You're learning to untangle your thoughts. You're cultivating an even mind.

As you begin to meditate, the default mode network (DMN) lights up. This is part of your monkey mind. Regrets, sorrows and fears may arise. This network has been shown to turn *down* in expert meditators. These folks are more able (from lots of practice) to stay with present moment thoughts. Someone with anxious feelings may have their DMN turned *up*, more than average. In this case there may be more fears, sorrows and regrets than is typical. This is one way meditation can help you manage anxiety. It can strengthen and tone this network (and connections to it from other parts of the brain) to stay present and not drift into worrisome thoughts.

Take Your Mind to the Gym

Practice paying attention. Choose a set time and pay attention to your chosen object of focus. It's like taking your mind to the gym. It's a fitness routine that will keep your mind healthy for life.

At first, you may not like it so much. There are so many thoughts! As a beginner, your mind wanders…a lot. But you may also like it right away. When I teach kids how to meditate, they tell me they really enjoy being guided into a still, quiet space within. Notice when you've lost attention. Then, with loving kindness, bring your attention back to your chosen point of focus. You're training your mind to sit and stay, like a puppy.

Check out the online resources for a guided meditation. You can also find several apps to guide you. Or, have someone read this list below to you the first few times you try it, until it becomes familiar and you can do it on your own.

Here's one way to do it:

- Set a timer for two minutes
- Sit comfortably (tall and relaxed)
- Gently lift your heart
- Close your eyes (if that's comfortable for you, otherwise gaze at the floor in front of you)
- Notice your breath
- Watch your breath rise and fall
- Just watch…nothing to do, nowhere to go
- Your mind will drift, when you notice, come back to your breath
- Keep watching your breath and refocusing when your mind wanders again and again for two minutes

Meditation is like medicine for your mind. You can do it when you don't feel great. As you go on with your awesome life, you'll start to do it before you don't feel great. This is preventative and it's totally the way to go. As a young person, if you do this, you will have a tremendous advantage in life. Plus, you'll feel better every day.

You're learning to say "hello" to the thoughts but not get into a story or conversation with them. Begin to notice your thoughts, as you do with the Body Scan Meet & Greet from Chapter 2. Be friendly and curious.

It reminds me of the movie, *How to Tame Your Dragon*. Who could be friends with a dragon?! Hiccup, the main character, was interested in understanding the dragons. Although he wasn't sure how to do it, he started paying attention to the wild dragon he caught. It was rumored to be fierce and dangerous. But Hiccup was patient and compassionate and was able to befriend a dragon. He even got to ride on the dragon and have amazing adventures. Begin to nurture your mind and you too will be on your way to amazing adventures.

Swap it Out

Now that you know a bit more about thoughts, what can you do about it? Thoughts are energy and each thought has a quality of energy. You can feel it in your body. Negative thoughts weigh you down. Positive thoughts are light and energizing.

You can't be aware of and direct each thought. But, you can start a trend. The quality of thoughts in your mind directly relates to the quality of your life. Over time, you'll be more familiar with noticing your thoughts. As you do, whenever a negative thought pops up (a worry, a meanness, a fear, a judgment) catch it and flip it. Trade the negative thought for a positive one. Stop the negative thoughts as soon as you notice and think something opposite.

~ ~ ~

Liza tried this before a test at school. As she sat at her desk, anxious feelings started to flood her body. It was a torrent of worry. Her palms started sweating, she felt ill. But she knew what to do. First, she softened her belly and that helped her breathe better. She put her hands on her belly and let her breath open up. Then, she noticed her thoughts, "I'm going to fail. This test is going to be hard. I'm not prepared. How will this affect my grades, my future, my life?!" Then, she started cultivating the opposite. "It's okay. It's just one test. I did study and I will do my best. This test doesn't define me. I've got this." And she kept breathing slow and even. Guess what? Not only did she pass the test, she got a B. That was the best grade she'd gotten so far that year in school. She was proud of herself not just because of the grade but also because she was the pilot, instead of the passenger. She took care of herself. Then, went out with her family to get rainbow sherbet to celebrate.

~ ~ ~

Since there are so many thoughts and so many are negative, this task can feel overwhelming. Here's a riddle: How do you change a cotton cloth to silk? One thread at a time. Pull one thread of cotton out and replace it with a thread of silk. Then, pull another cotton thread out and replace it too. Do it in baby steps, one thread at a time.

Slowly over time, you will notice your thoughts more and more. You'll catch yourself thinking something negative and you can swap it for a new, positive thought. You can trade it in for an opposite thought. When you've done this several times, it will become more familiar and you'll do it more often. It becomes a positive habit in your life. The cotton cloth of your habitual thoughts, which had been mostly negative and repetitive, will become like a luxurious shimmering silk cloth of positive creativity.

Workable Worry

It can be helpful to categorize your worry thoughts. Ask yourself if this is something you can do something about soon, like today or tomorrow. Worried about a test? Go study. Worried that you may be getting sick? Drink more water, get more sleep, take care of yourself. When you start to worry about something, ask yourself, "Is this a workable worry? Is this something I can do something about right now or within a day?" If yes, do it. If not, swap it out for a positive thought, take a walk in nature or take a nap.

~ ~ ~

Jackson learned how to do this like he learned to notice feelings of anger as sensations in his body (described in Chapter 2). He plays basketball and he was worried about an upcoming game. It was a loose worry jangling around in his mind. It's what I call a "blanket worry". It covered the whole situation. We sat down and talked about it. When he paid attention, he found the worry was about not playing his best and letting his teammates down. And this worry was about not being accepted by his friends. There can be many layers to worries. Was this a "workable worry" that Jackson had? Yes. He could practice, get a good night's sleep before game day and drink plenty of water. This would all help him play his best. He got out from under the "blanket worry" and stepped up to the captain's bridge. He took care of what he could do something about. And let go of the rest. His team ended up losing that game, but he felt like he played his best. He also felt inspired to keep practicing so he could do even better next game.

Jackson was also worried about the social unrest going on in his city and in the world. He overhears his parents talk about it and on the news they watch. It would keep him up at night thinking about it. There were so many angles to consider, so many intense emotions. Jackson has a big heart and he wanted to help. Is this a workable worry? An issue at the level of society or the world is not something a seven-year-old can or should try to solve. So, no. This is not a workable worry.

~ ~ ~

103

Lots of kids worry about world events and want to help! This can be a big source of anxious feelings. What to do? With something like this, try "Swap It". Think about something positive going on in your neighborhood or in the world. You may be able to get involved in some local activities where you can help. Something as simple as putting a positive sign in your window for neighbors walking by to see. Or, volunteer to pick up trash at the park, read to dogs at the shelter, or serve food to those in need. Worrying about something you can't do anything about soon isn't helpful for you or the situation you want to solve. It's hard and I see your sensitive heart. But to stay healthy, be clear about what's a workable worry. Then, use all these tools you're learning to shift out of anxious and into awesome.

This is a good place to revisit perfectionism. Is what you're trying to achieve workable? Two phrases I use when trying something very challenging, like writing a book, are "good enough" and "done is better than perfect".

Askfirmation

Your brain loves to solve puzzles. Asking a question for your brain is like throwing a ball for your dog. Your brain runs off all excited to retrieve the answer. It brings it back to you wagging its tail, tongue hanging out the side of its mouth.

Making statements can be very helpful. You're telling your brain what's true. I've shared several examples in the book. Writing or saying what you want to be true is one way to train your mind towards more positive thoughts. These are called "affirmations". These statements are best said in positive present moment terms. This means saying what you want, not what you don't want. "I feel calm." vs. "I don't want to be anxious!" And, saying it as it is in this moment. To your brain, everything is right now.

So, when you put something off in the future with words like "may" or "I hope", it keeps it out in the future.

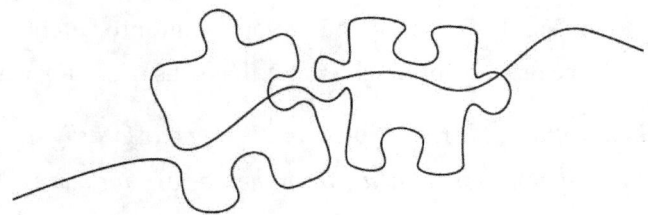

Sometimes though, with a statement, there can be some pressure. Your mind may start to struggle with "Is this really true, or not?" With a question, you're just throwing a ball.

A statement is like, "I feel awesome and can handle anxious feelings." If that feels good to you, go with it. If you doubt it, try a question like, "Why is it so easy for me to handle anxious feelings?" Your brain goes to work right away to filter for ways you easily handle anxious feelings. You can also ask, "Why is it so easy for me to feel calm at this time?" Your mind will start solving for "calm". You can call this an "askfirmation".

While we're on words we use, be careful of "my" as in "my anxiety". Anxious feelings don't own you. And you don't have to own your anxious feelings if you don't want to. It's visiting you, it's happening but it's not you. Instead of saying, "my anxiety," you could say, "this anxiety" or, "anxious feelings I'm having right now".

The Worry Witch

So many worry thoughts! Wouldn't it be nice to drop them off in a basket for someone else to take care of? You can, with the Worry Witch. You'll find an audio file of this guided visualization in the online resources. Or, have someone read this script to you. If you're not into witches, you can visit a worry tree or some other character that's just right for you.

Lie back in a comfortable resting position. With your feet slightly wider than your hips, palms up, out away from the side of your body.

Feel your whole body relax.

Feel the weight of your heels on the floor.

Feel the weight of the back of the legs on the floor. Feel the weight of your hips, your back and your shoulder blades on the floor.

Feel the weight of the back of the hands, back of the arms, and back of the head.

Feel the whole body heavy, soft and relaxed.

Tune in to the natural rise and fall of your own breath.

Breathing in as your belly expands. Breathing out as your belly settles back.

Breathing in and out – in and out.

Imagine you find yourself in a beautiful forest. This forest feels very friendly, and you can feel the light streaming in through the trees. You walk along the path through this forest and you feel the soft earth beneath your feet. You walk along until you come to a clearing and there you see a gate. The gate is part way open and next to it sits a silly looking lady. She has silver sparkles in her hair and she is wearing a pink polka-

dotted dress. She looks up at you with a silly smile and bright sparkling eyes. This is the Worry Witch. The Worry Witch is stitching. She has a quilt on her lap that she stitches and stitches. Next to her is a big basket full of fabric scraps and who knows what else. You walk up to the Worry Witch and she tells you that, because she is the Worry Witch, you can leave in her basket all of your worries – anything that has been bothering you, has you feeling sad or scared or worried – you can just put it right in that basket. The Worry Witch will use it to stitch into her beautiful quilt.

You leave all your worries with the Worry Witch, and you enter through the open gate. You look around and see a wonderful place. It feels familiar – like you have been here before. You look around and notice what you see. And you listen to what you hear. You smell and maybe even taste what's in this special place. Notice what it feels like in your body to be here. This is a special place just for you. And here you can relax completely without any worries or concerns. Here you are free to be who you truly are – full of peace, joy, and love. You now have a minute to relax and enjoy this place completely.

PAUSE

After having had all the time you need to relax, it's time to come back. You look around one more time and know you can come back to this special place any time by remembering what this place looks like, sounds like, smells like and feels like. You walk back out through the gate and see the Worry Witch there stitching away – crafting a magical quilt out of all the worries she has been given. You wave goodbye and she flashes you a silly smile as her sparkling eyes shine. You walk down the path, through the forest, feeling your feet on the forest floor and the light shining through the trees. You walk along until you find yourself resting right here.

Become aware of the room that you're in now.

Feel your body on the floor and feel your breath.

Slowly begin to wiggle your toes and fingers.

Move and stretch slowly and roll off to your side. Rest there a moment before rolling up to sitting. Notice how you feel.

Take a Nap

When all else fails, take a nap. This is sound advice from people who've studied napping. There are powerful messages in our society about the value of being busy. Napping can be seen as laziness but it's actually a powerful neuro technique. That just means it's good for your brain. Falling asleep for even a few minutes is like hitting your computer's restart button. It's a restart button for your brain. This is what Einstein and Edison understood.

Thank you to the scientists who discovered the default mode network and made naps a legit strategy for feeling awesome AND developing more creativity and calm. That's kinda part of feeling awesome, right?

My wish for you is that you get interested in the mind like I did when I was young. Your mind is a beautiful instrument. Make time every day to practice and learn how to use it to orchestrate your awesome life.

Body. Breath. Mind. This is how you take care of you. But it's not just you. You live in the natural world with other people. So, in the next two chapters, we'll look at how to be aware and connected in the world.

Captain's Log

Chapter 5 – Nature

"Nature never hurries, and yet everything is accomplished."

~ Lao Tzu

As you may have guessed, I love the word "awesome". I use it all the time. Once I said it to a friend and he said, "Awesome is for God and mountains." It's true. All of nature evokes awe. Nature is incredibly healing for the mind and the body. There are many reasons for this. First, nature has a routine. She changes her seasons, in order, every year, and the sun comes up on schedule every day. The earth turns in perfect balance. Also, flowers are flowers and trees are trees. They're not caught up in comparison or a busy schedule. A blue flower doesn't wish to be a red one. A tulip doesn't long to be a rose. It feels nourishing and uplifting to spend time in nature. Another reason is that the trees, flowers, and bees fully inhabit their purpose. They are expressing their true nature without any worry. All this reflects back your true nature and that feels good.

The slow and sure routine of nature is an antidote to our hectic lives.

The slow and sure routine of nature is an antidote to our hectic lives. Nature isn't anxious. Flowers aren't worried about who is friends with them. Lizards don't care what they look like. Trees are rooted firmly to the ground. They can teach us how to stay grounded too. Rivers are flowing. The water is not clinging to the banks trying to keep things the same because they are familiar. The river trusts the journey, even when it gets turbulent. Nature makes sense.

It was on my grandparents' farm in Iowa that I understood how much being in nature helped me feel less anxious. My sister and I would run through fields of corn that grew just above our heads, pick fresh strawberries from the garden and play in the yard with the chickens. My mind felt clearer and I was happier. I brought that sense of wonder and awareness back home to the sunflowers growing behind the garage and the lilac bushes that bordered our yard. As an adult, I still love to connect to nature in my own backyard. I sway in my hammock and peek at the blue sky through the spruce tree branches while my dog chases squirrels. Connecting with nature is a lifelong practice.

You might not have a backyard. Lots of kids I worked with in Chicago lived in apartments. Nature lives in the city too. You might have to look closer to find it. Parks with trees and perhaps a small pond or a stream. Gardens filled with flowers and the fragrance that wafts from them. Community gardens with vegetables in a variety of colors … green peas, dark purple eggplant, red peppers. Or a window box bursting with life. Even grass growing through a crack in the cement can remind you of your connection.

Even grass growing through a crack in the cement can remind you of your connection.

Connection to nature is important for overall wellbeing. Give yourself a treat. Get off the screen and out among the bugs. Here are some suggestions to get started. It's your nature menu. Choose the ones that seem delicious to you! You can try them all. But you don't have to. There may be one activity that helps you feel less anxious that you love to do over and over. Some kids find they need to do several in a row to feel relief. You can also discover your own way to connect with the natural world. These are my favorite nature connecting activities.

More than enjoyable things to do outside, these are ways to manage your anxious feelings. When your mind is racing like a Formula 1 car or it feels like a hive of bees has been let loose in your brain, nature can help quiet your mind.

Let's Get Science-y!

I don't need proof that nature is awesome. I always feel better when I'm connecting with the five elements of earth, water, fire, air and space. I LOVE to be in nature. You probably do too. But this is captain training, so let's talk about the science.

In Japan, doctors prescribe time in forested areas. It's called "Shinrin-yoku", or forest bathing. They've done a lot of research on the benefits. A study was published in 2010 in the *Environmental Health and Preventative Medicine* journal. The results show that forest environments:

- Promote lower concentrations of cortisol
- Lower pulse rate
- Lower blood pressure
- Increase parasympathetic nerve activity
- Lower sympathetic nerve activity

Cortisol is a stress chemical in your body. You learned that less sympathetic activity means less stress. Greater parasympathetic activity means more relaxation.

There are brain benefits too. Being with nature is one of the ways you can calm the alarm center in your brain. It can also help your pre-frontal cortex develop. This leads to better decision-making skills. How important is that?

Chronic stress and anxious feelings can weaken your immune system – the system that helps your body stay healthy. The germs in dirt help your immune system get stronger. A gradual exposure to allergens outside when you're young can also help reduce the chances of getting allergies when you're older. So, for your health, please squish your toes in the dirt and make mud pies (sorry if this makes your parents cringe).

Humans and plants evolved together. We have a lot in common. The plants in nature emit chemicals called aromatic compounds. This is what makes flowers, trees and fruit smell so good. These compounds are like medicine. In fact, medicine comes from plants. Modern medicine takes parts of these compounds and makes synthetic replications in the lab. For all time before this was possible, people used plants for medicine. This is probably one reason doctors prescribe forest bathing. Here's another fun science-y fact:

Your lungs are shaped like trees, upside down.

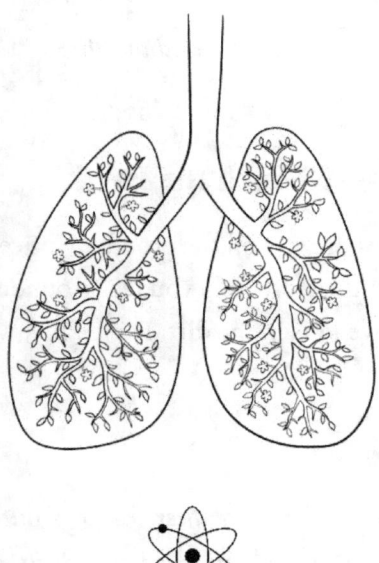

Breathe with Trees

Trees exhale oxygen and inhale carbon dioxide. You know that you breathe oxygen in and breathe carbon dioxide out. It's a perfect pair. We literally cannot live without trees. Thank you trees! Trees are your breathing buddies. This is one reason why being in a forest feels so good. Next time you pass a tree, take a deep breath in and a long breath out. The tree will thank you.

Around me the trees stir in their leaves

and call out, "Stay awhile."

The light flows from their branches.

And they call again, "It's simple," they say,

"and you too have come

into the world to do this, to go easy, to be filled

with light, and to shine.

~Mary Oliver

Touch the Earth

Go outside. Put your bare feet on the ground. Notice the connection you have to the earth. Let the earth help you feel grounded. You benefit from microbes and negative ions in the dirt. Do it daily, weather permitting.

~ ~ ~

Sam does this. No matter the weather, he goes outside barefoot and it grounds him. One time he was concerned about getting sick. He has lots of anxious feelings about throwing up. His stomach hurt, he felt shaky and his thoughts raced. He paced outside for several minutes until he calmed. He went back inside and then outside again, and back and forth for about ten minutes. After he did this, he felt much calmer, more grounded and more in control of his feelings.

~ ~ ~

Gardening is a fantastic activity to help you feel connected to nature. Whether in your own garden or walking down a street, you can talk to the plants, the bugs, the dirt. I like to compliment all the trees and flowers in my yard. "You are my favorite flower, you are my favorite tree." (I say that to all of them). Do this and notice how you feel. Develop a relationship with the elements of nature.

Flower Focus

Ralph Waldo Emerson said, "The earth laughs in flowers." He also said, "All life is an experiment. The more experiments you make the better." Try this experiment with the flowers that grow in your garden, in public parks, along neighborhood streets, or wild in the field.

Find a flower. Don't pick it! Leave it to live out its full life cycle and share its beauty with all who may pass by. Get eye level with this flower and get comfortable. Feel your breath in your body as you gaze gently at the flower. Try not to look away. Give this flower your full attention. Notice the texture and shape of the petals, how each one is similar to or different from the others. Notice how the colors on it blend and shift. What is at its center? What kind of leaves and stem does it have? Let it show you its flower-ness. Let the flower show you your essence too. Rather than seeing it just with your physical eyes, meet the flower's energy with your energy. Everything and anything can help you realize your own true nature. Why not let it be a fresh flower in full bloom?

Keep gazing at this flower as you breathe and relax your body. Do this for as long as you like. You can do this with anything in nature. A bug, a leaf, a tree, a stone.

~ ~ ~

It was several months of attending Anxious to Awesome™ classes before Olivia had any interest in these nature tools. It was all she could do to open up her breath and her body. One day, the weather was so nice, we decided to practice outside. I asked Olivia if she had ever talked to a flower. She laughed. "No, I barely talk to the other kids in my class" was her reply. Olivia had social anxiety. She felt awkward and unsure of herself. We'd spent a lot of time together and had developed a good relationship, so she was open to trying my suggestion of this Flower Focus tool. Something surprising happened. She laid a mat down on the ground near a patch of wildflowers. She rested on her belly with her elbows on the ground and her chin on her fists. I guided her through this activity, like an adult can do for you by reading the above paragraph. Then, I let her be quiet for some time. She seemed to drift off into a daydream. Then, we ended our practice time together with a guided relaxation and afterwards talked about her experience. She had a hard time explaining how she felt, but she knew she had a new understanding of herself. She felt bigger. Not like Alice in Wonderland who ate an "Eat Me" cake and grew enormous. She just felt like she had more room for herself. She had felt small and contracted, almost like she was trying to disappear. This insight with a flower gave her a different perspective of herself that lasted.

~ ~ ~

Sky Gazing

Find a place where you can lie down outside. Relax your body and your breath and begin to gaze at the clear blue sky. It's best if there aren't a lot of buildings in your view and never ever look directly at or near the sun. It's too strong and can harm your eyes. Let your eyes soften as you take in the great expanse of blue. Notice any clouds that drift by too. Gazing at the sky is like shaking the Etch-A-Sketch of your mind to clear the impressions. Do it for 20 minutes for best effect. I like to do this when my mind is really feeling scrambled or I'm overwhelmed with a decision. Nature gets to decide when you do this one. If it's cloudy or raining, pick another activity until the next blue sky.

Of course, you can do this at night with the stars too! Learn the constellations in your area. Watch them move through the year as the earth spins around in space. This is how captains have navigated their ships.

Nature Collage

There is a beautiful retreat center on Paradise Island in The Bahamas. I go there to share these wellness tools with families. We spend most of our time outside. We love to create a nature collage. This is how we do it. Children get time to explore the retreat center. They pick up a collection of found items from nature:

- Rocks
- Twigs
- Leaves
- Seedpods
- Feathers
- Shells
- Grasses

We then get together on a thatch-covered wood platform and each child gets a piece of paper. On it, they arrange the found nature items in beautiful designs. When done, we invite guests at the retreat center to come by and admire the creations, like a mini art show. Then, the kids carry the papers filled with objects to the edge of the platform. They tip their papers over the edge and let the pieces of their designs slide off the paper and right back to nature.

Try it yourself. Find items in nature (be mindful to take only what has fallen and in small quantity). Use glue on paper or simply place the found objects in a design. When done, you can return it all back to nature. Or, you can hang it in your home to remind you of your connection to nature. You can make a circular design with your nature items. This is called a mandala. Visit the online resources to see pictures.

You may also want to make a sculpture of found items in nature. Stack rocks or build twigs into an interesting shape. If you've made sand castles at the beach before, you already have experience with nature sculptures. Use found objects from nature as a brush for paint. Use mud as your paint! If you want to be wowed and inspired with nature collages, watch *Rivers and Tides*. This movie is about artist Andy Goldsworthy who uses nature to make art.

Sound Map

One of my favorite outdoor activities is to create a "Sound Map". Sit quietly with a piece of paper and drawing utensil. This paper represents the area around you. When you hear a bird heard chirping in a tree off to the left, make a mark that represents that bird in the upper left area of the paper. Several dark lines can represent the sharp "caw" of a crow. Swirly lines may show the "cheer, cheer, cheer" of a cardinal. Thick lines across the center of the page can show cars swooshing by on the street in front of you. You can draw that frog croaking over in the pond or just make marks to represent its croak.

This wonderful mindfulness practice can last 10 or 20 minutes. The longer you listen, the more layers of sound will be revealed. Share the sound map you have created with your nature companion. Come back to the same area later. Compare the sound maps. How much has changed in this same area?

~ ~ ~

I did this with Devon and his nine-year-old brother. They both had a lot of energy and their mom was feeling exasperated. We didn't have any paper, so we just listened. They tuned in right away. At first, they shouted out what they could hear and then we naturally settled in to silence. After a few moments we heard some more sounds and compared what one had heard to what another had heard. This calmed them down quite a bit and allowed them to get a good feeling for the park that we visited that day.

~ ~ ~

Nature Self-Portrait

When you can't be in nature, you can imagine yourself in nature. Draw yourself as a tree, a body of water, a butterfly or other winged creature, or as any element in nature. You may want to draw yourself as a flower after focusing on one for a time.

Animal Advocacy

Pick an animal you are interested in. For me, that would be a sloth or a dolphin or a cat. If this animal could talk, what would it have to say? Write from the perspective of the animal, like you're a reporter interviewing the animal. Where does it live? What does it like to eat? What would this animal want people to know about him?

My sloth would say, "s l o w d o w n".

Sometimes, when I'm feeling anxious, I feel like the world is caving in around me. It's a tight, small feeling. When I explore another perspective, it helps to open my world again. I don't feel so alone. Thinking about what an animal wants and does brightens my heart a bit. Try it and see how it feels for you. Write their story in your captain's log.

Essential Oils Are Nature in a Bottle

Bring plant power into your home with essential oils. Your emotional brain (the limbic system) used to be called the "nose brain". This is because the olfactory system (your ability to smell) is in this area of the brain. This is why smells are so strongly related to memories and emotions. You can use yummy smells to improve your mood and emotions. Citrus oils like lemon and orange are especially cheery and uplifting. Tree oils like frankincense and cedarwood can help you feel rooted and stable. Essential oils from flowers like lavender and rose can be calming and soothing.

~ ~ ~

This was the first thing Hannah tried when she got the brain tumor diagnosis. She was already anxious at school and the diagnosis increased her anxious feelings – a lot. Lavender, frankincense and wild orange were her favorites. Her mom would massage her hands and feet with these oils before bed. She also made a rollerball blend of oils to keep in her bag. At school she could dab some on her wrists and the back of her neck to help shift her mood.

~ ~ ~

Sam uses peppermint oil every day to calm his worry thoughts, his nerves and his stomach.

~ ~ ~

Remember your brain filter? It filters based on what comes in through your senses, except smell. Smell goes right to your monkey mind, your emotional brain. Essential oils can help shift you out of anxious feelings fast.

If you love things like essential oils and crystals, that's you being drawn to nature's healing wisdom.

If you love things like essential oils and crystals, that's you being drawn to nature's healing wisdom. Visit the online resources for more information on where to get the best quality oils and how to use them in your home.

Eat Nature

How close to nature is the food you eat? An apple that's fallen from a tree in your region has a lot of nature's energy - and nutrition. This is a huge topic and there are many factors to consider, so I can't advise you specifically. The food you eat does influence your brain and your mind. I call it mood food. Some foods leave you feeling yukky. Other foods help you feel energized, balanced and calm. Use your Body Scan tool in Chapter 2 to learn how different food feels to you. Consider how eating food from nature helps you feel connected to nature...and more awesome. Grab an apple when you have the choice. Do the best you can, that's all you need to do.

Live in Tune

Living in tune with the cycles of nature has a powerful impact on your wellbeing. Get up with the sun and go to bed when it's dark, as much as possible. Artificial light confuses the cycles in the brain. This is why too much screen time doesn't feel great. While this may not be practical to do all the time (like going to bed at 5:30pm in the winter in Minnesota), it's one aspect to consider when anxious feelings ramp up.

When the seasons change, change with it. As summer turns to fall, routine becomes more important. It can counteract all the turbulence in nature. Keep warm by bundling up and eat warm foods like soups, stews and roasted vegetables. As nature wakes up in the springtime, get moving. More physical activity and lighter foods help you transition out of winter hibernation.

There is a beautiful science of living in tune with the cycles of nature. It's very old, it's from India and it's called *Ayurveda*. It means "knowledge of life". The main teaching is to bring in the gentle opposites. It makes sense. When you're cold, you grab a blanket and put on socks to warm up. When you're hot, eat cooling foods like mint and cucumber. Start paying attention to nature around you and your own nature with in you. Feeling connected to nature is powerful medicine.

There is a strong message in our culture to "Hurry!" and, "Do More!" Nature is a wonderful antidote to all this. Being in nature helps you feel less stress because nature isn't stressed out. There is a deep truth to the rhythms of nature and just being in it helps you find your own rhythms. When connecting with nature, notice the sensations in your body. How do you feel in nature?

Which activities are you most excited to try? I love to see what kids create in nature. Send me a picture or tag me on social media. Contact information in the online resources.

Captain's Log

Chapter 6 – People

"Being good to people is a wonderful legacy to leave behind."

~ Taylor Swift

C an I admit to you a secret love for easy listening 70s music? It travels one of those well-worn neural roads in my brain. These songs are alllll about people, connections and love.

Songs like, "You've Got a friend" by Carole King, "You Are The Sunshine of My Life" by Stevie Wonder and, "Lean On Me" by my absolute favorite – Bill Withers.

Humans are social creatures, hard-wired to connect. Back in the cave-people days, connection to others meant survival. It's still true today. This is why it feels so terrible to be left out of a group or be rejected by others. That primal robot part of your brain wants you to be in a group of people for safety. Your monkey mind just loves to have friends! We need people in our lives to feel safe, have fun and better understand ourselves.

Today, there's more interaction than ever through electronic devices and yet you may feel less connected than ever. You're not alone in feeling alone. Isolation and loneliness are an epidemic.

~   ~   ~

Hannah had lost connection with her friends when her classes changed. She shared, "My anxiety and depression got really bad in 8th grade." But it's when she was struggling that she discovered she had true friends. She discovered her new friends were on her side. They helped her through it. She felt a lot more accepted.

Remember when she got a C on her math test? She was very upset and started having a panic attack. A friend saw her leave to go to the bathroom and texted her "Can I help?" Hannah replied "yes" so this friend went into the bathroom to help her. "I wasn't able to handle it on my own" she recalled. With help from her friend she said, "I felt better almost immediately."

~   ~   ~

Let's Get Science-y!

Studies conducted at the National Center for Biotechnology Information (NCBI) looked at the benefits of being with others on mental and emotional wellbeing. The research paper suggests that, "Social contact appears to have a very positive influence on the psychological and the physiological aspects of social animals, including human beings." Psychological = mind. Physiological = body. Specifically, that socializing reduces stress hormones in the body helping us feel less anxious. This is called "social buffering". The people in your life can reduce, or buffer, how intensely you feel stressful situations. This same report found, "Solitude itself can be a stressor to social mammals and they may show a high stress response when socially isolated." Hello, 2020. The whole world faced more than a year of social isolation. Being with others, in whatever way you can, is an important strategy for your wellbeing. Plus, it's awesome to have great friends. If you, like me, struggle with friendships, that's okay. My favorite humans are my mom and my sister. I get the benefits of social contact with them. Or, like Hannah, you may have friends you don't realize are friends – yet. You'll find your people. I'll share some tips to help.

Okay, a little more science. Remember that your amygdala in your monkey brain can be overactive and lead to more than average anxious feelings? This same part of your brain also reads emotional cues. That overactive part can make it seem that people are less friendly than they really are. Your brain is on high alert for threats and may see someone as a threat or unfriendly when they just have a neutral expression. This can make it harder to socialize and make friends. Use the tools in this book to help calm this part of your brain. It can help you find a better friend and be a better friend.

Safe & Social

You now know that your nervous system has a stress mode and a rest mode. Safety is the basis of communication. At the level of your biology, you connect when you feel safe. If either person has their alarm system activated, it will be hard to connect. Ask yourself, "Where is this person in their nervous system – stress or rest?" You can ask this of yourself too. It may be hard to tell. The breath is a good clue. Short shallow breathing = stress. Slow even breathing = rest. Your beautiful brain is wired to detect danger or safety and can do so from facial and vocal cues. You can develop the ability to internalize the feeling of safety, which allows you to feel connected. From here you can be more social. It's who you are, but it's often disrupted by anxious feelings.

Another person can help you move into a feeling of safety. The instinctive part of your brain recognizes calm from facial features. A smile, crinkly eyes and a slightly tilted head are read as safety. The brain knows this person isn't a threat. When you're feeling anxious, another person can help you feel calmer with a calm demeanor. You can do this for others too. Calm is contagious. Slow even breathing is contagious too.

Belonging

Your heart has unlimited power to give and receive love. To forgive yourself and others. To be compassionate, too – from the kid at school who called you a name to the dog who ate your homework. Giving and receiving love is good medicine. And, love is unlimited. The more you give away, the more you have.

Giving and receiving love is good medicine.

The NCBI study mentioned above also found that when you're with a group of people you enjoy AND you're doing something to help others, it can reduce chronic disease. Being with people is good medicine. Being with people while you're helping others, is *really* good medicine.

As an added bonus, good friends are a lot like chocolate. An article published in the 2017 BMC Neuroscience Journal reported that cooperating with others has been shown to light up the reward centers in the brain. The same area that lights up from the pleasure of eating chocolate.

Maybe you've felt left out, forgotten, discounted, or even threatened because of the way you look, what you can do, how you express yourself, what you believe, or where you live. This can be a major source of anxiety. Nobody wins when anyone is left out. I just want to say, "I see you."

Friends, family and community. Shine your flashlight of awareness on these relationships. Pay closer attention to people and you will naturally feel more connection with them. Use your tools to feel calm so you can better connect. This probably isn't news to you, but hugs are also healing. A firm hug promotes the calming function of the nervous system.

None of this important human interaction happens through emojis on your phone. You need people, in person, and now you know why.

Social Anxiety

We talked about The Great Pause. Holding your breath can strengthen your breathing system for better breathing habits. That can reduce anxiety. We also talked about breath holding as a symptom of anxiety. Socializing is kinda like this. Being with other people can help you feel less anxious. It can also cause anxious feelings.

This is one I can speak to from experience. I've dealt with social anxiety by not socializing! It felt easier than trying to negotiate all the nuances of being in a group. When I am out with friends and that overwhelming feeling starts to rise up in me, I would walk out of the party, the beach gathering, or whatever was going on. I imagine others thought I was rude or something like that.

As I practiced being more aware of how I felt inside, I learned to enjoy socializing and also learned when I needed to take a break. I've learned to manage the feeling of my gut starting to fall in on itself while people stand around and say goodbye…for hours, like we do in Minnesota.

Here's what I do. First, I notice the feeling. It starts out as a tightening in my gut and a fidgeting feeling. I've learned this is my nervous system getting ready to fleeeee. In the past, that fleeing feeling would swoosh me out the door before I even noticed what had happened.

Now, I notice. Then, I accept. I allow it to be what it is. Then, I breathe. My stomach has tightened up and I realize I'm not really breathing so I start to soften my abdomen and let the air flow. I relax my face and smile. This also sends a message to my brain. Finally, I tell myself I'm going to be okay. "Mira, you're fine. You've got this." And then I'm able to say all the "good-byes" with warm and friendly feelings.

Try it:
- Notice
- Accept
- Breathe
- Smile
- Affirm
- Repeat until the feeling passes

This works for many anxious situations. It works even better when you have a daily routine of connecting to and being aware of your body, breath, mind, nature and people. It can help prevent anxious feelings in the first place and also puts you in a better place to deal with it when it does happen.

Let's Talk

Communication with others is what makes being in relationships so interesting! Clear communication can be challenging. You've learned that each person has their own filters and may see the same situation differently than you. Good communication comes down to learning to listen well. The mindfulness you practice with your own breath or a flower, can also be done with another person. Get curious about the person with whom you're talking. Instead of thinking about what you'll say next, stay with what they're saying. There's a magical phrase that can help you keep listening. It's, "Tell me more about that." You can also say something as simple as, "Oh, yeah?" to keep the channel open. Try it with a friend and see what happens.

Mirroring

We play a fun game in the Anxious to Awesome™ classes called Mirroring. Mirroring is the basis of communication. It helps players get comfortable exchanging eye contact, facial expressions and body postures. When you sync up with someone like this, you develop rapport – a good connection. Plus, it's really fun and funny.

- Two kids sit facing each other (or stand)
- One is the mirror
- The other does whatever they like – facial expressions, hand movements, whole body movements
- The "mirror" mirrors all this back
- After a time, switch who is the mirror
- Option: don't declare who the mirror is and mirror back and forth spontaneously

~   ~   ~

Liza attends a school that has a great program for kids who are deaf and hard of hearing. She and the other kids in this program communicate using American Sign Language (ASL). We had a lot of fun with this Mirroring game. This game and other tools in the book helped them manage their anxious feelings. Liza and her peers have added stress at school because of the strong focus on verbal communication. The kids in this program taught me so much about communication during the two years I worked with them. It's way more than words. In fact, words are estimated to be only about 7% of how we communicate. The rest is body language, facial cues, eye contact, hand gestures and vocal tone. Ultimately, communication and connection happens through the heart, not the head.

~   ~   ~

Seen & Understood

This is nice to do with a family member or a very close person in your life. Looking into someone's eyes for more than a few seconds is a very intimate experience.

- Sit facing your partner. Take a moment to get comfortable and let your breath settle. Then, both of you hold your left hand out, palm facing up. Hold your right hand out, palm down. Rest your right hand on your partner's up-turned left hand. Let them place their right hand on your up-turned left hand. Think: left = receive, right = give.

- Look into each other's eyes, trying not to blink too much. Coordinate breathing.

- After gazing for a few moments, close eyes and send warm love, energy or light from your heart through your right hand into their left as they send to you in the same way. Accept the love and energy they are sending you. Feel who your partner is and feel who you really are.

This exercise helps you see and feel the truth of the other person while allowing yourself to be seen and known. You may wish to share what this experience was like with your partner. This may be something you do after an argument to get reconnected, or before an important conversation.

These two tools, Mirroring and Seen & Understood, can help improve your communication skills, which helps you connect better. Human connection is a great antidote to anxious feelings.

Selfless Service

Helping others helps yourself. It feels good to share a smile, open the door for someone or help them carry something heavy, whether that's their groceries or their heavy heart from having to say goodbye to their beloved orange cat.

When I feel anxious, it can feel overwhelming to think about how to help others. I can barely take care of myself! It's a two-way street. Sometimes you'll need people to look out for you. Other times, you'll be there for someone else. As with many tools in this book, you can practice when you're feeling less anxious. It becomes a natural part of what you do and who you are. It can keep anxious feelings at bay.

Do something for someone without them knowing about it. Just because you know it will help them and it feels good to help. It can improve confidence and self-esteem while reducing stress. Helping others has also been shown to reduce pain! Ironically, helping is even more beneficial when you don't do it for yourself – for the benefits you'll get, but instead with a focus on others. It doesn't matter if you get paid for what you do or not. It's about your intention – why you're doing it. Let go of the outcome, whether that's money, a reward or a shout out on social media. This is what makes the helping so healing.

Thank You Cards

You can say "thank you" out loud, or silently in your mind. Anytime. You can even write a thank you card. If you're like me, you may worry that you don't know what to say or how to say it. The person receiving the card won't care too much exactly what you say, but they'll be thrilled to their toes to have received it. Especially your elders. Especially in these days of instant communication.

Take your flashlight of awareness and shine it on another human being. They will blossom like a flower in the midday sun. You are simply saying, "I see you." You can even write that on the card. Seeing and being seen is what humans are made for. Remember we talked about the source of anxious feelings being a sense of disconnection. There are so many ways to connect with others.

You get to decide with whom you connect. You can make eye contact as you pass someone in the grocery store, and smile. But if it doesn't feel right, don't do it. Remember we talked about body sensations and how your body talks to you? Listen to your body signals and you'll know when it feels right to connect with others in your community by smiling and saying, "Hi". You can try these tools to connect just with the people you know and like best.

You are energy and everyone around you is energy. Just like you may not want to talk with someone, you may not want to interact with someone's energy. You can make a shield with your imagination to feel protected and safe.

Star Shield

This is a guided visualization. You can do it seated or lying down. Find a quiet place where you won't be distracted and get comfortable. Have someone read this part to you, (or make a recording for yourself):

Let your body relax and feel your breath flowing in and out. Experience yourself standing outside on a beautiful star-lit night. Gaze at the stars in the sky. One star stands out for you, and you recognize this as your star shield. Leap up into the sky and grab that star. Once you have it, land safely back on the ground. Hold your star in front of you. Feel the light. What does this star feel like to you?

You can shape this light into a shield. However you want it to be. It can be as big as or even bigger than your whole body. It could be tiny, like a charm that rests on your heart.

Once you have a feeling for your shield, you can activate it anytime, anywhere. Experience yourself jumping up to grab your star and bring this light down in front of and all around you when you want to activate it.

I imagine stars to be warm and huge, like a blanket. I know that I can create a blanket sort of shield with this star's qualities. Sometimes I see my one star expanding and brightening with its golden light. I like to imagine sculpting it into a useful shield shape for me. This is just one suggestion to inspire your own creative ideas. You may want to make a shield woven of oak tree branches or spider webs or fairy wings. Your self-understanding is growing every day. You've got what it takes to do this.

People all around the world are more like you than different from you. Look for common interests and shared purpose. Let's live in a world of connection. We can all help anxiety NOT be the number one mental health challenge in the world.

Captain's Log

Chapter 7 – Practice

"You miss 100% of the shots you don't take."

~ Wayne Gretzky

All right captain, time to set sail. You have many tools in this guidebook to help you feel more connected to and aware of your body, breath, mind, nature and the people in your life. Choose one tool from each area to practice every day – or most days. This is your workbook for self-awareness and self-regulation. Mark it up, dog-ear pages, come back to it again and again. Use your captain's log.

Pick your favorite tools and activities from this book, the ones which have you exclaiming, "Oh, ya, I need that!", or "Ooh, that would be fun!" Try it for a few weeks until it becomes familiar and routine. Then, add a few more. Keep practicing. It's like learning to crochet or play the French horn. It may feel awkward or difficult at first. Keep trying. You'll get the hang of it. Soon you'll find your flow. You were made for great things.

When you cook, you prepare by getting your ingredients and tools together, the sauce, the pasta and the pan. When you play a game, you get your uniform on, tie your shoes and get your equipment. When you play a saxophone, you put the reed into the mouthpiece and place the sheet music on the stand. You wouldn't start cooking or playing a sport or practicing your saxophone without getting ready. You couldn't! Do the same for your day. Get ready to create your day – to play your day – every day.

Together, we're going to set up a daily routine. This helps keep your ship on course. It keeps you from crashing into the rocks, drifting off course or running your ship aground.

There are two ways to use the tools in this book. The first way is called "formal practice". In this chapter, I'll show you how to set up a special place, and how to pick a set of tools to do at a certain time and place each day.

One form of anxiety is obsessive compulsive disorder (OCD). It could be that the need for routine is amped up. In this case, be careful to understand why your child is going through a certain routine and how it feels when they do it. Routines are nurturing and help someone feel safe. They'll feel good after a morning routine where they brush teeth, eat a good breakfast and take the dog for a walk. If this routine feels like a burden or that it has to be done so something bad doesn't happen, then it may not be a helpful routine. You can ask, "Is this working for me, or against me?"

The other way is "on-the-go". You'll learn some tools by heart or use slips of paper to remind you. Then, choose one to do anytime when you want to feel less anxious and more awesome.

Bringing your boat to the dock for regular maintenance is like the formal practice. Adjusting the sails as you go is like the on-the-go practice. You can use the same tools for either situation. This is where you'll put this practice into your life:

- In the morning
- After school
- Before bed
- On-the-go, throughout the day

Up to you how much time you spend. I love five-minute breaks. That's all it takes to develop these lovely routines in life. Less is more to start.

It takes about 21 days for your brain to form a habit. The new skill is being learned in your wise brain. Then, it moves to the automation/robot part in about 21 days. That's three weeks. I like knowing this. It helps me feel more patient with the process of learning something new. I hope it helps you too.

When you're feeling anxious you may also feel overwhelmed. It's hard to make a decision about what to do in this state. This is why we're making a plan together. I've listed every tool you can literally whip out and do in less than five minutes. These are your on-the-go strategies. Take little pieces of paper and write a tool on each one. Put these paper pieces into a jar or a bowl. This is your Awesome Tools Jar. You can even organize each activity type by color – body is yellow, breath is blue, nature is green for example. Visit the online resources for a sheet with the tools already listed for you to print and cut up.

BODY	BREATH	MIND	NATURE	PEOPLE
Name It!	Crocodile Breath	Mind Gym	Breathe with Trees	Mirror
Meet & Greet	Buddy Breathing	Swap it Out	Touch the Earth	Seen & Understood
5,4,3,2,1	Balloon Breath	Askfirmation	Flower Focus	Service
Cow/Cat Mouse/Dog	Breathing Wings	The Worry Witch	Sky Gazing	Thank You Cards
Hello Sun	The Great Pause	Take a Nap	Nature Collage	Star Shield
Super Star	Square Breath		Sound Map	
Triangle	Turtle in a Shell		Nature Self-Portrait	
Tree	Plug into the Earth		Animal Advocacy	
Eagle	Whole World		Essential Oils	
Twist	Heart Flower			
Tense & Release				
Ears & Toes Massage				
Family Dance Party				

When needed, grab a piece of paper and do what's written on it. Whew. If you'd like, do another. Sometimes, you need to do several tools in a row to find relief. Anytime, anywhere. Ask a friend or family member to join you or do it on your own. My cat, Sita, likes to do these activities with me. She sometimes sits on my lap when I meditate (take my mind to the gym). My dog, Boudica, loves the sound map in nature. And yes, I have included pictures of my pets in the online resources.

You can also take these pieces of paper with one tool on each one and make a schedule. Pick one from each category and put them in an order you like to start the day or for an afterschool reset. Tape them to the bathroom mirror or pin them on the kitchen bulletin board. Refresh your list every few weeks or months.

You learned about why your brain loves routine. Sameness equals safe to your robot brain. When you're feeling more anxious or know you'll be in a stressful situation, routine is even more important. When you're feeling awesome, you may want to be more spontaneous. Your fancy, modern pre-frontal cortex and emotional brain love that!

Dedicated Practice

About 1500 years ago a wise person, named Patanjali, wrote a guidebook for developing awareness and connection. He understood how to manage the mind. He also understood the importance of a dedicated practice. Dedicated means that you do it consistently over a long period of time, without a break and with a lot of love.

Dedicated means that you do it consistently over a long period of time, without a break and with a lot of love.

He even understood what might get in the way of a dedicated practice. He wrote a list. Disease, boredom, doubt, distraction, laziness, cravings, ignorance, failure to make progress and slipping back from the progress made. Ugh. Has anything like this ever gotten in the way of your staying with something new or something hard? Everyone just said, "Yes."

When you are sick or bored, when you doubt yourself or get distracted, when you feel lazy or desire to do something else, when you don't understand, don't make progress or lose the progress you've made you're not likely to keep practicing the tools that help you. Now you too know these obstacles. Don't let them get in the way of feeling awesome.

A planned (formal) practice helps keep these things from getting in the way of your progress. Because if you keep at it, you move past these obstacles. It also helps you get back to your plan when you fall off. Isn't it reassuring to know that these obstacles are common to all of us?

Use one of the tools in this book and you'll likely feel better right away. Use them every day, and you're changing the course of your life. You're on the road to awesome. This is a dedicated practice.

I've recommended your own captain's log to record your journey. Use your captain's log if you've made one. What's working? What's not? What do you want more of and less of? Make a plan, shift your routine and be sure to include unstructured free time every day. Write it down. Choose one day a week to create and revise your routine. I like to do this on a Sunday afternoon. I call it the Sunday Setup. Nature can guide you here too. The change of seasons is a great time to refine and recommit to your habits. There are four times a year when you can sit down and review – at the change of each season. Your routine may change with the seasons or the school year.

Drift is a thing. You may find yourself falling off or drifting away from your new habit. Slowly, overtime, you can end up far off course if you're not paying attention. That's all right. It happens – a lot. Just begin again.

You can drift way from a habit and begin again a thousand times. Starting again is part of the practice. It doesn't have to be perfect.

Have you ever watched a baby learn to walk? Up, one step, boom, on the ground. They fall again and again trying. They don't give up. A baby won't say, "Walking is hard, I quit!" They just get back up and try again every time until they learn to walk. Scientists have measured this. An article was published online October 19, 2012, titled, "How Do You Learn to Walk? Thousands of Steps and Dozens of Falls Per Day." In it, they reported emerging walkers fell an average of 17 times an hour.

Creating and sticking with a routine feels daunting for many families. Sam's mom doubted her ability to commit and practice regularly. It was easier when she understood the obstacles, drift and baby steps. Having a record of your journey can also help you look back to reflect and make a plan going forward. This is what your captain's log is for.

Here are some examples of daily routines and rituals from other awesome kids.

~ ~ ~

In addition to challenges with her health and school, Hannah's parents were getting a divorce. Her mom wanted to help her with anxious feelings and learned the tools in this book. Her mom also had anxious feelings and they both use the breathing tools quite often. When Hannah thinks she's going to have a panic attack, she does long, slow breathing and it usually keeps her from having one. She still uses her essential oils. This is when she and her mom can connect at the end of the day and they both cherish this time. They're also a part of her routine getting ready for school. She knows when she needs to ramp up her self-care skills. School is still a challenge, but her grades are good and she's able to go each day, without anxiety.

~ ~ ~

Riley knows that using her mudras and paying attention to her breath gets her ready to face a challenging situation. She puts her hands into a certain shape to help her transition from one situation to the next. She loves Turtle in a Shell best. This sends a message to her brain – "I'm safe." It takes just a minute and it gives her the confidence she needs. She does this to start each day, in her room, before breakfast. She also makes some positive statements to herself, like, "I've got this." and "Today is going to be a great day."

~ ~ ~

Jackson's parents like these tools and find it helps them to feel more awesome too. They've created a morning routine as a family. Getting the family to all land in the same place at the same time during the busy morning routine is no small feat. So, they make it a game. Dad sets a gong timer on his phone. It gongs ten times. The game is to be sitting in their Special Place before the last gong. Sometimes Jackson is racing in at the last gong, with his cat tangled up in his feet as he runs in. Other days, he slowly drags his feet and his bedraggled stuffed toy from when he was little into the space and waits for his parents to join. His sister sometimes gets to the Special Place a few minutes early and does a few morning stretches. Dad likes to join her. He says it helps his back feel less sore during the day if he has taken a moment in the morning to stretch.

They gather in the Special Place they created as a family. Jackson's mom plays soft gentle music she enjoys and they set the timer for three minutes. Some days family members are in a mood for this and some days they are not. But they know the benefit of this ritual, so they've made the *commitment. They keep each other accountable. Everyone starts the day from a good space of awareness and connection.*

~ ~ ~

Sam's practice is mostly on-the-go tools. His parents, teachers and aids all know these tools and they help Sam choose something to do as needed. He makes minor adjustments throughout the day so he doesn't drift too far toward the rocky shores of anxious feelings. Sam likes to twist so his teacher has the whole class twist and stretch before starting a lesson.

~ ~ ~

Olivia and her family like the Sunday Setup. They have more time for practice and planning. They pick some ideas from their Joy Jar and Awesome Tools Jar and schedule them in for an after-school reset. Olivia's mom also prepares a few healthy snacks for the kids to enjoy after their short reset practice. Olivia and her sister still do five minutes of morning stretches on school days.

~ ~ ~

Here are a few specific routines for you to follow.

Good Morning Routine – 5 minutes

- Body Scan
- Cow/Cat/Mouse/Dog
- Easy Twist
- Turtle in a Shell
- Askfirmations

Good Morning Routine – 15 minutes

- Inhale or apply wild orange essential oil
- Breathing Wings
- Hello Sun – three to six rounds
- Super Star and/or Triangle
- Easy Twist
- Meet & Greet Body Scan
- Pick a Mudra
- Take Your Mind to the Gym

After School Reset

- Breathe with Trees on your way home if you are walking
- Crocodile
- Cow/Cat/Mouse/Dog
- Heart Flower Mudra
- Seen & Understood with your favorite person
- Captain's log on feelings from the day

Sweet Sleeps

- Balloon Breath – racing and restless thoughts can keep you from a good night's sleep, so imagine all the stressful stuff from the day being deflated from your balloon as you flutter to the ground
- Write in your captain's Log
- Cat/Cow
- Tense & Release
- Body Scan Meet & Greet
- Lavender oil foot massage

If you wake up in the middle of the night, use essential oils, deep breathing, Swap It! And/or Askfirmations like, "Why is it so easy for me to drift back to sleep?"

Before a Test or Big Game

- Askfirmations – "Why is this test/big game so easy for me?"
- Hello Sun – with the whole team before a game
- Cat/Cow – in your desk sitting up
- Square Breath
- Eagle

Sunday Setup

- Make a Stress-O-Meter
- Take a walk and Sky Gaze
- Help a friend or neighbor
- Review your captain's log and plan for the week
- Nap

Baby Steps

Small changes made slowly over time lead to awesome outcomes. Don't try to change too much too fast. That's stressful! You've learned that your brain loves familiarity and habit. The alarm goes off when there are lots of changes – even good ones. One way to add some new habits to your routine is called "habit stacking". You stack a new habit onto or next to one you already have. You already brush your teeth, right? When brushing your teeth, notice your thoughts and see if there are any negative ones you can swap out for positive. Or, focus on slow deep breathing.

If you walk to school or to the bus, you can pick a nature tool to do on the way, like Breathe with Trees or imagine yourself as the bird singing from the sign post.

Make a commitment to these tools each week. You'll start to see how, with small adjustments, you can incorporate these life-affirming practices into your daily routine. It may feel like a struggle at first. But when done slowly, with attention and commitment, habits that don't help you begin to fall away. In time, you'll look back and see that big changes have taken place, which felt like baby steps all along the way.

Unstructured Free Time

There's a structure to our society – a routine – that may not be true for you. There seems to be this belief that we need to get somewhere from here. Where we already are isn't good enough. Where we need to go is better. And the worst part is, we're late in getting there! There is a "hurry up" culture all around. Do more, achieve more. Have you felt it? It can be a source of anxious feelings – big time. You can excel and achieve, in balance. Now that you're more aware and connected, pay more attention to your schedule. What's being asked of you and to what are you saying "yes"? How does it feel in your body? Do your activities and commitments leave you feeling more anxious or more awesome? Your brain loves unstructured free time just as much as routine. We need both! Rather than cramming your schedule full of things to do, consider free time an important part of your schedule. Have "white space" on your calendar. Chunks of time when nothing is scheduled. This is spontaneous free time structured into your routine.

Consider free time an important part of your schedule.

Joy Jar

What brings you joy? And how often do you do it? This may not be an easy question to answer. Life can feel full of "have tos" that drown out the "want tos".

What do you love to do? Make a list. I'll start.

- Sway in my hammock
- Read a book (book + hammock = bonus joy)
- Watch the sunset color the whole sky
- Sip a cool fizzy drink
- Play with my dog
- Nap with my cat
- Make soup from scratch
- Write in my journal
- Hike through the woods
- Swim, kayak, tube - anything in the water
- See live music (bonus if it's outside and I can dance barefoot in the grass)
- Explore a new city

- Ride my bike
- See fireworks

Riding my bike through an interesting neighborhood to see music outside is a joy explosion for me. If there are fireworks after the music and I went swimming that afternoon, I've probably just had the best day of my life.

Make a list of what you enjoy. Include simple things you can do anytime for free, like reading a book in the hammock out back, as well as bigger things that cost money and need to be planned, like going to your local amusement park.

Kids tend to have loads of computer-based activities. I'm going to challenge you to find things offline that you enjoy. There's enough time to be on the computer. Balance it with screen-free fun.

It's okay if this list starts out small. Start to pay attention to what brings you joy. My nephew took my mom, his kids and me to a trampoline park. Wow! That was fun. I didn't know to include "trampoline park" in my Joy Jar. It's in there now. This is something that needs to be planned out and costs money. I also really enjoy going to a local bookstore to poke through the books and talk to the people who work there. I can do this anytime and it's free.

Now look back over your list. How often do you do these things? Some are not daily activities. Maybe you have something on your list that you can do once or twice a year. But what about watching the sunset? It happens every day everywhere and it's free. If it's something that brings you joy, why not do it every day? Build your life around what you love. It's easy to get distracted. That's why I like to have a jar or basket full of reminders. I call it a Joy Jar. Set it somewhere next to something else you grab every day, like your toothbrush, skateboard or backpack. Remind yourself of what you love. Do something you love every day. This is what life is for. If you'd like to share a picture of your Joy Jar or some of the things on your list, I'd love to see it.

This can be the same jar as your Awesome Tools Jar, or a different one. Write things you love to do on a piece of paper, decorate them if you like, and throw them into a jar or box. You can decorate this too, if that's something you enjoy.

We have a pond nearby. It's like a zoo! We always see something interesting. Blue herons live there. We saw an owl once at dusk. There's a muskrat in the pond who swims around like he is the boss of that place. There's also a troupe of turtles basking in the sun on logs. We often don't notice them until, "plop, plop, plop", one by one they drop into the water to find safety from the puppy at the end of our leash romping up to greet them. That all brings me joy. Sometimes I get lost in the rush of the day or a low mood or worried feelings. My Joy Jar jolts me out of it. "Oh, ya" I'll think to myself when I pluck out the piece of paper that has "POND" written on it, "I love to walk around the pond." I go do it and feel a whole lot better.

Pick a piece from your Joy Jar when planning the weekly schedule and be sure to get something you love to do on your calendar. You can also walk by and grab something from the jar anytime for spontaneous inspiration.

I know kids who have felt so anxious, they didn't even want to grab something from their Joy Jar. The mind is on lockdown. This is why it's so important to have your daily routine. It makes your mind more flexible and stronger. So, if at first you feel resistant to things – even really good things, know that you're not alone in this. Also know that you can change it so it's not always going to be that way.

A Special Place

You are amazing. There's a reason you're here. You have important work to do. Your work – your purpose – is to discover who you are and share it with the world. That's it! There's only one you and there will only ever be one you. Who you are is unique and what you have to offer is essential for the full expression of humanity. Whoa! Don't worry. It will come to you as you grow and explore and learn who and how you are.

Self-discovery deserves a special place. YOU deserve a special place. This is a place in your home that is quiet and peaceful. It's a place dedicated to self-discovery and self-mastery. A place for formal practice. This helps you be more aware of who you are and helps you get better and better at being your wise self.

There may be one special place in your home for the whole family to use, or you may have a special place in your own room – just for you.

Some families have an altar with formal religious symbols to inspire this time of quiet self-reflection. Other families have a table with a candle, a beautiful stone and a simple clear vase for a fresh flower. Other families have a corner filled with pillows and drawing supplies. Depending on your climate and setting, your special place could be outside in the garden or even in a treehouse.

Suggestions for a special place:

- Uplifting & inspiring images. This could be a religious figure, a famous humanitarian (no movie or rock stars, please!) or a family member. It could be a beautiful design or abstract art.
- Something from nature. A stone, leaf, flower or crystal.
- A candle (please be very careful with an open flame and be sure an adult is present, or you can use a battery-operated candle).
- A simple timer, bell or chime.
- Affirmation cards, a notebook and pen, an inspiring book, coloring supplies. You can read, write or draw inspiration.
- Something to place it all on. I've used a cardboard box covered in cloth. Or, it could be an exquisite hand-carved wooden table.

- Comfy seating. This could be a chair, cushions on the floor or a folded blanket.

A special place is dedicated to quiet contemplation. There's no rough-housing or arguing in this space. No card games or homework. Over time, this place becomes filled with positive, calm and quiet energy. As soon as you sit down here your brain and body are triggered to settle into a peaceful state. It's like a pocket of calm. Protect it.

So, what do you DO in your special place? It's not so much to "do" as it is to "be". I recommend sitting here every day for five minutes. Do this as a family if you can coordinate schedules, or each one individually as schedules allow. There are some tools in this book you can do here. You can pick a morning routine and do it here. This is also a lovely place for quiet at the end of the day. These few minutes help you train your mind to be strong and focused, open and creative. This is what this whole book is about. Do it every day, whether you feel like it or not. Just like brushing your teeth. You will be amazed at the quality of peace and clarity that lives within you.

Maybe you don't have your own room, like me when I was a kid. Or there's just a lot going on where you live and there might not be a just-right place for this. Use your imagination to create your special place. When I travel, I carry a small box or a bag with some of these special items tucked inside. Then, wherever I am, I can find a place to sit and lay out the things that remind my mind of calm. I use some tools, like take my mind to the gym or practice mudras. When I'm done, I put the items back in their bag and tuck it away until the next time. You could even carry a special stone in your pocket to remind you that you always have a special place wherever you go.

You know about formal practice and practicing on-the-go. You understand some important things about practicing and where to do it. You've seen what other kids do on a daily basis and now, you're ready to have your own daily practice of being your awesome best self. You're ready to captain this ship on the amazing adventure that is your life.

Captain's Log

Chapter 8 – Everyday Awesome

"Tension is who you think you should be, relaxation is who you are."

~ Chinese Proverb

I'd like to introduce you to "everyday awesome". This doesn't mean you won't ever feel anxious again. It means you have what it takes to be with anxious feelings and not be overwhelmed by them. You have the tools to shift your mind and mood. You're connected and aware.

You've learned about your nervous system and the brilliance of your body making sure you stay safe and stay alive. You've also learned many ways to feel less anxious and more awesome. Feelings are messages and anxious feelings are a message that something big is going on. Pay attention, breathe, and take care of yourself like you know how to do. Ask for a break, be brave, trust yourself.

Ask for a break, be brave, trust yourself.

You're okay, just as you are – with or without anxious feelings. Anxiety is one of many guests at this party called life. Be a polite host and find out why anxiety has dropped in for a visit, but don't let anxiety bully the other guests at the party.

You know how to scan your body for messages. Your breath is more familiar to you than ever. You've got a nice relationship with nature as well as friends and family. You're like a young neuroscientist with how much you now understand about the workings of your brain and mind. It's like the instrumentation on the dashboard of a plane, and you have earned your wings.

The Hero's Journey

A professor named Joseph Campbell studied mythology across all cultures for all time. He found something amazing. All the stories had one theme. He called this theme, The Hero's Journey. It's also called the monomyth – one story. It seems that every culture wanted to understand their lives better and had stories, or myths, to help. Everyone told the same story. That means this is your story too.

What is a hero? A hero is an ordinary person in a challenging situation who takes action. The hero's journey has three main stages. First, the hero is living in the ordinary world and is called to an adventure (like the journey from anxious to awesome). The hero is hesitant at first, but with a nudge, begins the adventure. Then, the hero faces challenges, learns a great deal and develops qualities and skills along the way (just like you're doing with these tools). Cool guides and mentors also show up to help. The hero faces a huge challenge, like slaying a dragon (or anxiety), conquers it and then returns home. The hero is transformed and shares what was gained on this adventure with people back home.

This is how Joseph Campbell describes it:

"A hero ventures forth from the world of common day into a region of supernatural wonder: fabulous forces are there encountered and a decisive victory is won: The hero comes back from this mysterious adventure with the power to bestow boons on his fellow man."

~   ~   ~

I shared this hero's journey story with Sam during one of our sessions together. We liked to practice in the basement surrounded by his vast collection of Star Wars figures and posters. Before we started, his mom told me she wanted him to go to summer camp, but he didn't want to go. He thought he wouldn't fit in and that the other kids would tease him for being different.

He was already interested in mythology, so he was pretty excited to hear about The Hero's Journey. After telling him the steps on the path, he recognized himself as that hero on the journey. At dinner that night, he told his mom he would go to summer camp.

~   ~   ~

Joseph Campbell said, "We have not even to risk the adventure alone; for the heroes of all time have gone before us; ...where we had thought to travel outward, we shall come to the center of our own existence. And where we had thought to be alone, we shall be with all the world." Deep, right?

This is the journey we've been on together. This guidebook is like a map. You are a hero and you're on the journey of life. When you know where you are on your journey, you'll feel less anxious. Like Sam on his way to summer camp, you may be at the initiation – the call to adventure. Or, you may be facing the dragon. Practice the tools you've learned, and you'll be like the hero who comes home with special gifts to share with family and friends.

One of the most popular movie series of all time is Star Wars. George Lucas, the creator of Star Wars, said Joseph Campbell's work influenced the structure of this series. You can also find the hero's journey in The Hobbit, Harry Potter and hundreds of other modern-day stories.

In Star Wars, Yoda is modeled after the ancient masters of wisdom. These are the wise mentors who show you the way and help you develop your skills. Luke Skywalker is a student just like you. Darth Vader is like anxious feelings. This is the major challenge the hero faces. The Force is the unseen energy that can be tapped and directed. In this movie series, when a character is facing a challenge, they are advised to "Feel The Force." You can feel The Force too.

Using the tools from this book can help you experience The Force. Talk to people in your family and ask them how they feel this energy. Consider this energy in your Special Place. Ask for guidance. Listen for a reply. Look for messages in your dreams, meditation and visions.

I like to think of it as an unconditionally loving intelligence.

I like to think of it as an unconditionally loving intelligence. Awareness of and connection to it is the root of wellbeing. Find The Force in your life. It's an inner sense of a living relationship to a higher power.

"There is a force within you that gives life. Seek that."

—Rumi

This subjective stuff is now being measured scientifically too, just like the mind science. The subtle realms are being explored like the ocean and outer space. Perhaps one day when you grow up, you'll be a scientist who studies the subtle energy that makes up all life.

> *In her book, The Spiritual Child, Lisa Miller, PhD shares that, "...research from the field of positive psychology shows that spiritual development is associated with positive emotions and qualities of thriving that include a sense of belonging, optimism, elevation, and connection to 'something larger' that gives purpose and meaning to life. There is nothing known to science as profoundly associated with thriving and success in our children." She also states that, "There are hundreds of rigorous elegant peer reviewed scientific articles that show spirituality as the root of wellness in the first two decades of life."*

The tools in this book create the conditions for you to be more connected to and aware of the essence of who you are. Some people call this soul or spirit. You may experience it in a mindful moment in nature, or while taking your mind to the gym. Or, looking into the eyes of someone who loves you a lot. Do you see how it all ties together so beautifully? Awareness is light. Light reveals the connection of all things.

Awareness is light. Light reveals the connection of all things.

Truth Test

At the beginning of the book, you learned how to create a Stress-O-Meter to get a sense of how anxious you are. You also have a way to measure the Truth. This meter is inside you. This is your "Truth Test". Instead of measuring anxious feelings, you measure if something feels true to you. It's another kind of inner compass. For me, I get goosebumps, or more often I get a feeling like I'm about to cry. This is a physical sensation that signals that what I'm doing or saying or thinking about is my Truth. What's your signal? Pay attention and you'll discover it. It could be a feeling in your body, an image that comes to mind or even a sound or voice you hear from within. Try the "Name it!" tool from Chapter 2 to discover some "truth" sensations in your body. Keep notes in your captain's log. Then you can use this inner Truth Test to help you make decisions to stay true to your own course.

We're living in topsy turvy times. Big events are changing the landscape of humanity. Anxiety is like the sea sickness you feel sailing these turbulent waters.

Unseen, beneath the surface, something holds you in place – where you are meant to be. This is self-trust, a belief in yourself, your faith. Faith is an anchor.

Keep it simple, sailor (K.I.S.S.). When life can be so complex and challenging, a simple solution is often best. Let it be easy. Let it be fun. Anxiety is a complex condition, and it may feel far from easy at times. A great ancient wise person, Lao Tzu, said, "The journey of 1,000 miles begins with a single step." Focus on the one step in front of you. Then another…and another…and another.

E – Everyday

A – Awareness

S – Soothes

Y - You

This is your guidebook to awesome. It's your user's manual for YOU. These tools are simple and free. You can do them anytime. You have the techniques and understanding to take care of yourself. You can go from anxious to awesome anytime anywhere. It doesn't need to be perfect. You can do this. You've learned so much. Each one of us is different and unique.

You'll discover your own ways of being with and moving through your anxious feelings. I'd love to hear what works for you! Go to the online resources to send me a message.

You and the children in your life have several tools you can use to facilitate the relaxation response in the body at the level of the nervous system. Remember, this is a physiological response – not something we convince ourselves of, but something to which our body and mind responds. I won't be the first one to remind you to take care of yourself so you can care for others. We've talked about how humans mirror each other. Anxiety is contagious in this way. If one family member is anxious, it's likely others are as well. Fill your cup. This is why I wrote this book for families, so everyone can feel better together.

Few students, even by the time they have reached high school, have developed effective plans for managing stress. This is your guidebook to developing these plans. In our experience, children are grateful when they are shown specific ways to relax. "Aaahhhhh," they say. "So, this is what it feels like, and now I know how to get here."

And now YOU know several ways to help the children in your life experience the benefits of stress-hardiness. Imagine your children traveling through life with better health and a greater sense of peace and self-mastery. It's a wonderful gift to share.

Safety Talk

I spent many years kayaking and rafting white water rivers around the world. Each trip started with a safety talk. The guides would remind us to be an active participant in our own rescue. Should we find ourselves bounced out of the raft and bobbing around in turbulent water, we can help getting helped. Keep your feet pointed downstream, look around, reach out or even swim over to something that's thrown towards you. These are all ways to be an active participant in our own rescue (versus curling up into a ball with eyes squeezed shut tight and crying out, "I want my mommy!" – which believe me, sometimes I was tempted to do). We were each being asked to be a hero – to take action in a challenging situation. Be an active participant in your own rescue. You are more powerful than you know.

Be an active participant in your own rescue. You are more powerful than you know.

Okay, sailor! You've got your compass and your map. You've got secret keys, a flashlight, spy glasses and a life jacket…so to speak. You can leave me off at the next port because you've got the resources you need to sail on. I've helped you steady your vessel for the high seas, just like my sister, Stephanie, steadied my bike until I was ready to balance on my own. You're ready to be the captain of your own ship, an active participant in your own rescue, a hero on this journey of life.

Life is awesome, and so are you. Part of the reason you are awesome is because of the wonderful, amazing neuroscience you now know and understand – and can influence. Your presence makes nature a better place and it makes the people in your life better too. There are a hundred other reasons you're awesome that I don't know just because we haven't met – yet.

You've got this. I believe in you. You were made for great things.

Captain's Log

Gratitude

It takes a village to raise a child, and to birth a book. These are the folks in my village who I greatly appreciate for their support in bringing this book into being.

First of all, I'd like to recognize and honor all the kids and families in my classes, workshops and individual sessions who've taken this journey from anxious to awesome. They've inspired me in so many ways with their brave, adventurous hearts. They have helped shape the contents of this book.

Gratitude to all my teachers and mentors, especially Joseph and Lilian Le Page as well as Richard Miller, Ph.D. Through their dedicated practice they were able to so beautifully articulate this wisdom for me which in turn allowed me to articulate it for you.

Gratitude to Dot Maver, who has been a spiritual mentor of mine since I was in high school and in some ways is the Godmother of this book. Gratitude to Heather Olstad for helping me develop my inner compass, and to Angela Bixby for her clarity and insight and for being a true soul sister.

Gratitude to the Get It Done Team. They are all genuine angels, teaching by example the power of generosity and kindness...and great writing.

Gratitude to the families who agreed to read the book in its development stages and gave invaluable feedback that helped shape it into being. Carla Pfahl, Toni King, Miranda Etzel, Mara Spiropoulos and families – thank you. A special thank you to Gabby and her mom, Shelley Russell.

Gratitude to Linda Brody and Amber Bloomquist, two of our most experienced Anxious to Awesome™ facilitators, who also gave valuable feedback on the book as it was being developed.

The strongest shape in the universe is a triangle. My triangle is made up of my mama and sister, Cheryl Binzen and Stephanie Schmit. We are a writing team. No words can express the honor, trust, respect and LOVE I have for these two women. I couldn't have chosen better family. This book would not exist without the countless hours they contributed to editing, formatting, deciding and a million other things that go into creating a published book.

Gratitude also to Steve, who patiently waited for me while I was consumed by this book and made pad Thai and spring rolls for Thanksgiving dinner while I spent the entire day writing.

And, gratitude to you, dear reader. Your willingness to become the captain of your own ship has an incredibly positive impact upon our world.

www.ingramcontent.com/pod-product-compliance
Lightning Source LLC
Chambersburg PA
CBHW060519130626
46553CB00002B/565